# Glorious
# COUNTRY

# Glorious
# COUNTRY

## Food
## Crafts
## Decorating

Liz Trigg · Tessa Evelegh
Stewart & Sally Walton

PHOTOGRAPHS BY

MICHELLE GARRETT AND JAMES DUNCAN

ACROPOLIS
EDITIONS

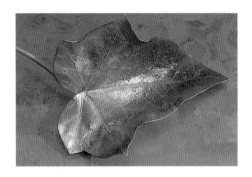

First published in 1995 by Lorenz Books

© Anness Publishing Limited 1995

Lorenz Books is an imprint of
Anness Publishing Limited
Boundary Row Studios
1 Boundary Row
London SE1 8HP

ISBN 1-85967-150-0

Distributed in Australia by Reed Books Australia

Distributed in Canada by Raincoast Books

A CIP catalogue record for this book is available from the British Library.

Publisher: Joanna Lorenz
Project editor: Lindsay Porter
Designer: Janet James
Photographer for Country Decorating: James Duncan
Stylist for Country Decorating: Tessa Evelegh
Photographer and Stylist for Country Crafts and
Flowers and Country Cooking: Michelle Garrett
Illustrator: Nadine Wickenden

Photographs on pp 6–9, 14, 15, 36, 37, 56 and 57
by Steve Tanner

Printed and bound in China

# Contents

# Country Style

Picture a house in the countryside on a bright autumn day, smoke wafting from the chimney into a brilliant blue sky. There are trees that have turned glorious shades of yellow and orange and there is a chill in the wind. Cats are asleep in shafts of sunlight, ignoring the birds that chatter on the rooftop. On a summer day, the arch over the gate will be covered with roses, and hollyhocks will stretch up the white walls past the open windows from which muslin billows out, caught by the warm breeze. ❧ Step inside the house and smell bread baking in the range; leave your boots on the rack and walk across the cool flagstones. Sink into a comfortable chair by the scrubbed pine table and look around at stencilled patterns, crocheted lace, gleaming copper pans and wooden spoons. This is the country that we see in our dreams, and if our waking hours are passed in a high-speed, high-pressure city environment, these dreams have an added seductive quality. Rosy images of the pastoral are potent symbols of a way of life that seems somehow gentler, less stressful and more natural than the urban routine. As the pressures of late twentieth-century living mount, we want to put some of that country tranquility back into our lives. One of the easiest ways of doing this is to recreate some elements of country style in the home, providing a restful and welcoming environment to come back to. You don't have to live in a cottage to create the cottage look: the look comes as much from a way of thinking as from a way of living. ❧ This book shows you how to get into that way of thinking, and how to channel it into creative projects that will bring something of the dream of country living into your home — whether that is a farmhouse or a flat. But it's not just the end-product of your creativity that you will value; in the process of designing and making country-style artefacts and effects you will find a satisfaction and sense of peace that are the real goals of country style.

BELOW: *The beautiful yet practical nature of patchwork is typical of country style.*

# Achieving a Country Look

Country style has many interpretations and all over the world there are towns-people who dream of a calmer way of life in a place where traffic doesn't bustle, food has more flavour and night skies are filled with stars, not neon. This may be an idealized picture, but it has an underlying truth: country life is still governed by seasonal changes, not man-made deadlines. ❧ Country homes are alive, growing and comfortable and country decorating is for living in, not just looking at. Many of the effects that we think of as talismans of country style have an eminently practical function. ❧ Country style may vary a

lot, according to nationality and the local climate, but there is a core of recognizable elements. It is a home-made, functional, comfortable style. There is often a big kitchen area, with a large scrubbed pine table and an assortment of comfortable chairs. Country kitchens can be a riot of pattern and colour, where the dresser is stacked with displays of china and the beams are hung with baskets full of drying flowers and herbs. Gleaming copper pots and pans should never be

ABOVE: *Although several motifs are present in this room, the restricted use of colour pulls the whole look together.*

hidden away in cupboards, so use butcher's hooks to display them out of 'head banging' reach. Floors need to be practical, tough and easy to keep clean, so floorboards, flagstones, linoleum or cork tiles are the favourite choices, and they can all be softened with washable cotton dhurries or rag rugs. ❧ The food prepared in the country kitchen is hearty and nourishing, and is prepared from the produce of the season — warming roasts and stews in the winter and light, fresh vegetable flans or fruit tarts in the summer. Locally grown produce — organic, if not from your own garden — will taste immeasurably better if it is a seasonal treat rather than a year-round staple. ❧ Through-out the home, flower arrangements take their cue from nature and are combined with other organic materials to provide a more casual, spontaneous look than hot-house blooms. A ginger jar that has been in the family for years stands alongside an enamel jug filled with flowers from yesterday's walk. You might choose to float flowerheads on a glass plate, or collect supple twigs to form a heart-shaped wreath wrapped with trailing ivy. The colours of autumn may be represented by gourds, vegetables and dried seedheads. ❧ The country house is not a fashion statement, and its colour schemes should reflect the natural colour in the landscape; these need not be dull, bland and safe; they can be as rich as autumn, with touches of brilliance, or warm as a summer pasture filled with buttercups or a field of ripe corn. ❧ The house responds to personal touches; a painted border may still be there in 50 years, so paint it thoughtfully. Make time in your life to be creative, whether it be with stencilling, floor-painting or embroidery. All home-made crafts add richness to the home and give you a sense of personal achievement that money cannot buy. ❧ There are step-by-step projects here to suit all levels of experience and creative ability. You may feel daunted by embroidery but more confident about making patterns in tin with a hammer and nail; unsure about flower arranging, but able to pop a few dried flowerheads into a terracotta pot.

*BELOW: Decorative panels can transform a piece of furniture. If you are not confident about painting free-hand, stencilling is a simpler option.*

Whatever you choose, rest assured that all the projects have been designed to give maximum effect for minimum effort. If you want to ring the changes very quickly on your walls, use a colour glaze with a foam-block print or stencilled border. Giving floorboards the limed look requires the hard work of sanding first, but the painting can be done and

COUNTRY STYLE

ABOVE: *Patchwork cushions soften a wooden chair, and provide a practical use for odd scraps and remnants of fabric.*

dried in an afternoon. If you have considered laying cork tiles, then stain half of them black and make a real impact with a chequer-board floor. 🐿 When it comes to choosing materials, or pieces of furniture to decorate, take a tip from the squirrel and start hoarding! There are so many second-hand stores, car boot sales and jumble sales around, and if you buy things that have potential, you will always have something to hand when the creative mood strikes. It can be amazingly difficult to find a wooden tray or a nice tin can when you want one, so have a 'potential' corner in the loft or the shed, and keep it well stocked! 🐿 On a very practical note, there has been a major change in materials for home-decorating recently, with the arrival of water-based paint products. There is no longer any need for solvents to clean brushes; they rinse out under the tap. The biggest bonus of this revolution is that decorating time has been cut in half. Water-based products dry very quickly, and this is especially useful when applying many coats of varnish to painted furniture. The rule to remember is not to mix oil and water, so if you tint varnish for an antique effect, mix acrylics with water-based clear varnish or oil colour with traditional varnish. 🐿 Whether you go for the total country look for your home, or just a few details, always try to decorate in a way that is sympathetic to the character and age of your house. Use the best features, like an interestingly shaped window, as focal points; be courageous about removing a ghastly fireplace, or disguising oppressively heavy beams. Your home should please you, and country style is about personal touches, natural materials, warmth and comfort. So, follow your instincts and enjoy the charm of country life.

# COUNTRY
# Decorating

## STEWART AND SALLY WALTON

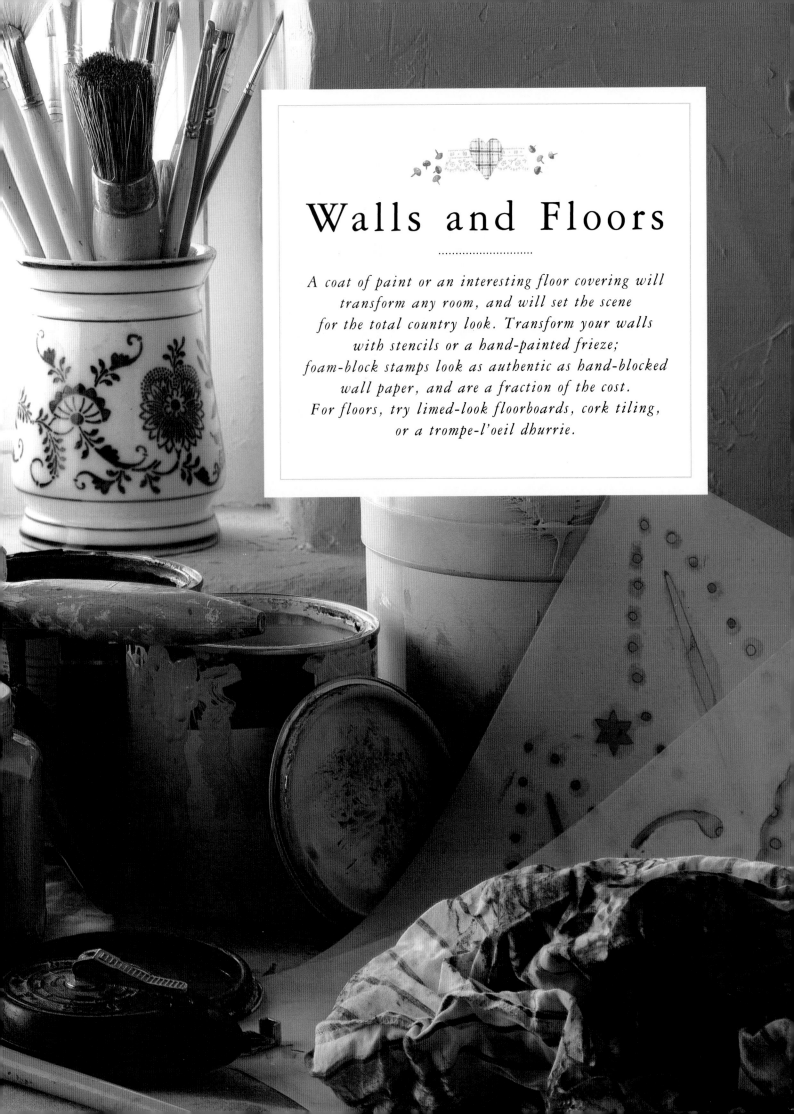

# Walls and Floors

A coat of paint or an interesting floor covering will
transform any room, and will set the scene
for the total country look. Transform your walls
with stencils or a hand-painted frieze;
foam-block stamps look as authentic as hand-blocked
wall paper, and are a fraction of the cost.
For floors, try limed-look floorboards, cork tiling,
or a trompe-l'oeil dhurrie.

# The Country Palette

Colour has a great influence on us: it can affect our moods quite dramatically. Choose your palette from nature's harmonies, avoiding artificially brilliant colours. It would be a mistake to think that natural colours are all shades of beige; just think of autumn and the huge variety of yellows, oranges and scarlets that mingle among the trees.

When painting the walls country-style it is best to avoid a perfect, even finish – go instead for a patchy, glowing, colour-washed effect. By doing this you can use strong colour, but in a transparent way that is not as heavy as solid colour. Don't avoid strong colours like brick red, deep green or dusky blue. The furniture, rugs, pictures, ornaments, cushions and curtains will all combine to absorb the strength of the wall colour and dilute its power. If your rooms are dark, use the strong colours below dado-rail height only, with a creamy, light colour on the upper walls and ceiling. Darker colours can be very cosy in a large room, but if you want a room to look bigger it would be best to stick to a lighter scheme, and use a stencil or free-hand border to add colour and interest.

If mixing your own paint is too daunting a prospect, you could go for one of the new 'historic' ranges made by specialist producers. These paints are a lot more expensive than ordinary brands, but the colour ranges are designed to harmonize with antiques, natural building materials and old textiles, and if your budget can stretch to them, they really are wonderful.

If your courage fails and you choose white walls, think about highlighting the woodwork. Paint a deep, rich colour on the skirtings and the window- and door-frames, allow it to dry and then

ABOVE: *Colours derived from nature are not necessarily sombre. Think of clear blue skies or a field of wildflowers.*

paint a light colour on top. Use a damp cloth to wipe off some of the topcoat, and sandpaper to lift colour that has dried. This will give you an effect of flashes of brilliance to add warmth to the room.

Choose natural colours that make you happy, and remember that country-style decorating is not about having everything matching. You don't need co-ordinating curtains, carpets and lampshades. On the contrary, the more eclectic the choice, the more stunning the effect can often be.

Giving your home the country look requires attention to the basics – the walls and floors. Get these right and the rest is easy. A bare room with powdery wall-paint, stencilling and a stripped, limed floor has a real country feeling, whereas no amount of folk artefacts and rustic furniture can transform to 'country' a tastefully wallpapered, corniced and thick-pile carpeted drawing room!

The ideal way to begin would be to clear the house, remove all the old wallpaper

and carpets and start from scratch, but this is a luxury that few can afford. It's more practical to think in terms of a room at a time, repainting the walls and adding one of the country-style floors that are featured in this chapter.

This chapter shows how the basic elements of a room can be changed to make it feel more individual. When you paint, stencil or print on your walls, they truly become your own, and this never happens with wallpaper, however good you are at hanging it! We sometimes suggest cheating a little: roughening up smooth surfaces, wiping off more paint than is put on, or stencilling unevenly, for a worn-away look. You can't wait a hundred years for this to occur naturally!

The ideas for the projects have been inspired by folk art and by real-life examples of country decorating of period homes. There has been a recent revival of interest in the subject and it is now possible to buy kits to age practically anything, with a plethora of equipment required for the job.

Whatever you choose for your walls and floor, it is important to see them in terms of a backdrop for your own tastes and possessions. Paintings, mirrors, lamps, plants, shelves, rugs and furniture will all add to the final effect. A painted border may appear to be too dominant in an empty room, but the effect will be much more subtle when the furnishings, accessories and personal details have been added.

Remember that country style is more about relaxation, comfort and harmony than precision and fashion; this is the type of decorating that is a pleasure to involve yourself in, so enjoy the process as well as the result.

CLOCKWISE FROM TOP LEFT: *The walls and floors have been coated with tinted varnish to simulate the patina of age.*
*Deep, brick red is bold, yet warm in a sitting room. The soft colours of this crazy patchwork quilt*
*are punctuated with vibrant stitching.*

# Brushed-out Colour Glaze

*This soft, patchy wall finish is pure country. It's traditionally achieved using either a very runny colour-wash, or an oil-based glaze tinted with oil colour, over eggshell paint. This project gives the same effect, but is easier to achieve.*

The unusual element in the glaze is wallpaper paste, which is mixed in the usual way before the addition of PVA glue. The wallpaper paste adds a translucency to the colour and the PVA seals the surface when dry. To tint the glaze you can use powder, gouache or acrylic paint, mixed with a small amount of water first, so that it blends easily.

Use a large decorator's brush to apply the glaze, dabbing glaze on to the wall about five times within an arm's reach. Then use light, random strokes to sweep the glaze across the area, to use up the dabs and cover the area. Move along the wall, blending each area with the next.

This is a very cheap way of painting a room, so you can afford to mix up more glaze than you will use, and throw some away. This is preferable to running out before you finish, because it is so difficult to match the original colour. A litre / 1¾ pints of glaze will cover almost 40 square metres / yards.

### MATERIALS

*PVA glue*
*wallpaper paste*
*acrylic, gouache or powder paint,*
*to colour the glaze*
*large decorator's brush*

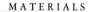

1

Prepare your wall-surface: ideally it should be an off-white vinyl silk, but any plain, light colour will do, if it is clean. Wash old paint with sugar soap and leave it to dry. Mix up the glaze, using 1 part PVA glue, 5 parts water and ¼ part wallpaper paste. Tint it with three 20 cm / 8 in squirts from an acrylic or gouache tube, or about 15 ml / 1 tbsp of powder paint. Vary the intensity of colour to your own taste. Experiment on scrap lining paper painted with the same background colour as your walls. Get the feel of the glaze and brush, and adjust the colour at this stage if necessary.

2

Begin applying the glaze in an area of the room that will be hidden by furniture or pictures; as your technique improves you will be painting the more obvious areas. Start near the top of the wall, dabbing glaze on with the brush and then sweeping it over the surface with random strokes, as described previously.

3

The effect is streaky and the brushstrokes do show, but they can be softened before they are completely dry. After about 5 minutes brush the surface lightly with your brush but don't use any glaze. The brush will pick up any surplus glaze on the surface and leave a softer, less streaky effect. When working on edges and corners, apply the glaze and then brush it away from the corner or edge. You will still find that the colour may be more concentrated in some places, but it will all look very different when the room is furnished.

# 'Powdery' Paint Finish for Walls

*You may need to 'rough-up' your walls a bit to achieve this look; this is easily done with a tub of filler, a spatula and some rough-grade sandpaper. Think of it as a reversal of the usual preparations!*

This paint finish imitates the opaque, soft colour and powdery bloom of distemper, the wall finish most used before the invention of emulsion paint. The joy of decorating with this 'powdery finish' paint, is that it can be used directly on concrete, plaster or plasterboard – indeed almost any surface – without lining paper or special undercoats. The paint is diluted with water, to the consistency required, and is slapped on with a large brush. Mistakes and runs can be wiped off with a damp cloth, and the paint is a pleasure to use. It takes about two hours to dry, and the colour lightens considerably as it does so, until the final effect is revealed – a soft powdery surface of matt colour that will bring instant warmth to any room.

The 'distressed' plaster effect has a charmingly country feel. Perhaps we imagine that real country folk didn't have the time or inclination to decorate to a perfect finish; for whatever reasons, there is something very comfortable about walls with irregular surfaces and faded paint.

### MATERIALS

*Polyfilla or similar filler
spatula
rough-grade sandpaper
Brats 'Mediterranean Palette'
paint in shade 'Asia'
large decorator's brush*

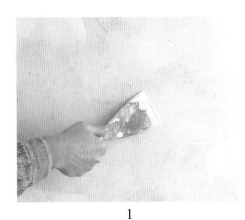

**1**

Prepare the walls by stripping off any wallpaper down to the bare plaster. Spread the filler irregularly with the spatula to simulate the uneven texture of old plaster. Use thin layers, applied randomly from different directions. Don't worry about overdoing the effect; you can always rub it back with sandpaper when it's dry, after about an hour.

**2**

Blend the dried filler into the original wall surface using the sandpaper, leaving rougher areas for a more obvious distressed effect. Mix the paint with water in the ratio 2 parts water to 1 part paint.

**3**

Begin painting at ceiling height. The paint is likely to splash a bit, so protect any surfaces with an old sheet or decorator's cloth. Use the paintbrush in a random way, rather than in straight lines, and expect a patchy effect – it will fade as the paint dries. The second coat needs to be stronger, so use less water in the mixture. Stir the paint well; it should have the consistency of single cream.

Apply the second coat in the same way, working the brush into any cracks or rough plaster areas. Two hours later the 'bloom' of the powdery finish will have appeared. The element of surprise makes decorating with this paint exciting, especially as the final texture is so mellow and effective at covering, but not concealing, the irregularities of the wall's surface. We used this surface as a base for the stencilled border on the following page.

# Stencilled Border

*Stencilling tends to spread around the house like a climbing plant, appearing round doorways and winding along picture rails, up staircases and across floors! It is a delightful and habit-forming activity and it's extremely difficult to be a minimalist when it comes to stencilling.*

The design used for this border came from a Rhode Island house that was built and decorated in the eighteenth century. Stencilling was an extremely popular means of decorating interiors, and stencils were used to create pillars and friezes as well as all-over patterns, with as many as seven different designs on a single wall.

A border design like this one is perfectly suited for use above a dado-rail, but there is no reason why you should not use it at picture-rail, or skirting-board height, or even as a frame around a window. Or you may not have a dado-rail but still like the effect of a wall divided in this way. In this case it is a simple matter of marking the division with paint or varnish.

Use a plumb-line and a long ruler to divide the wall, marking the line in pencil. The wall below the line can be painted a darker shade, or, if you are using the 'Mediterranean Palette' colour, a coat of clear satin varnish will darken the colour and add a sheen. The stencilled border will visually integrate the two sections of wall and soften the edges between them. If you vary the depth of stencilled colour, it will look naturally faded by time.

MATERIALS

*tracing paper*
*Mylar or stencil card*
*spray adhesive*
*scalpel or craft knife*
*masking tape*
*Brats Mediterranean Palette paint*
*in shade 'Asia' (optional)*
*varnish in shade 'Antique Pine'*
*household paintbrush*
*stencil paint*
*stencil brush*

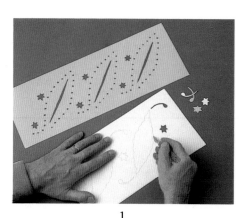

1

Trace and enlarge the pattern from the template section. Stick it on the Mylar using spray adhesive. Use a scalpel or craft knife to cut out the stencil carefully. Repair any mistakes with masking tape and always use a very sharp blade which will give you the most control when cutting. Peel off the remaining tracing paper.

2

If desired, prepare the powdery paint finish on the previous page, then paint the whole wall in 'Asia'. Paint the lower half of the wall with a coat of Antique Pine tinted varnish. Use random brush strokes for a rough finish.

### 3

Apply a light spray of adhesive to the back of
the stencil and leave it to dry for 5 minutes.
Position the stencil at a corner and paint the
first colour. Use the paint very sparingly,
wiping the brush on absorbent kitchen paper
before using it on the wall. You can always
go over a light area to darken it later, but
excess paint on the brush will cause blobs,
and bleed through to the back of the stencil.
Lift the stencil and wipe any excess paint
from the pattern edges before positioning it
alongside the stencilling. Continue along
the top of the dado-rail until the first colour
is complete.

### 4

Stencil paint is fast-drying, so you can
immediately begin to add the next colour,
starting at the same point as you did with the
first. Work your way around the border,
remembering to wipe the stencil clean
as you go.

# Free-hand Frieze with Half-gloss to Dado Height

*This project combines the idea of dividing up the wall with textures and colours, and the free-hand painting of a vine frieze. The frieze will take some planning and preparation to achieve the casual free-hand effect, but the finished painting will look effortless and be unique.*

A coat of gloss paint below the dado-rail will provide a practical, tough, wipe-clean surface where you most need it, and the gloss gives the colour a marvellous reflective shine. The lighter colour above the dado has a matt texture and the shade is reminiscent of cream straight from the dairy. If you don't have a dado-rail dividing your wall, this project is just as effective on a plain wall.

The secret of painting free-hand curves on a vertical surface, is to steady your hand on a mahlstick, which is quite simply a piece of dowel about 45 cm / 18 in long. Make a small pad of cotton wool at one end, cover it with a small square of cotton or muslin and secure it with a rubber band. Use the stick by pressing the pad against the wall with your spare hand, holding the stick free of the wall. Rest your brush hand lightly on it to prevent wobbles and jerks. Practise the curves with the mahlstick before starting the frieze, but remember that the charm of hand-painting is its variability, so relax and enjoy yourself.

## MATERIALS

*National Trust paint in shades
51 (Sudbury Yellow)
emulsion, 14 (Berrington Blue)
full gloss and 43 (Eating Room
Red) oil eggshell
paint-roller and tray
gloss-roller
2.5 cm / 1 in decorator's brush
masking tape,
if necessary
chalk line or ruler
chalk
stencil card with design*

*medium-weight card
scalpel or craft knife
1 cm / ½ in square-ended artist's
brush
gouache paint in Indian red and
raw sienna
45 cm / 18 in length of dowelling
(of pencil thickness)
small wad of cotton wool
square of cotton fabric
rubber band
number 6 round-ended artist's
brush*

#### 1

Apply yellow emulsion to the prepared wall
with the paint-roller, from ceiling to dado.
Paint blue gloss colour between the dado and
skirting, using the gloss-roller. Using the
red eggshell paint, and the 2.5 cm / 1 in
brush, paint the skirting board and the dado-
rail, if you have one. Use masking tape,
if necessary, to give a clean line. Use a
chalk line or ruler to draw light chalk guidelines, marking out the depth of the frieze.

#### 2

Using your chosen stencil, lightly mark
out the position of the frieze by drawing
through the stencil.

#### 3

Paint the thick and thin lines, using the
square-ended brush, flat and on its side, and
the gouache paints. To add variety to the
line, mix up two different shades of the same
colour and use both randomly.

#### 4

Make up your mahlstick as described
on the previous page.

#### 5

Paint in the curved stems, using the round-
ended brush and gouache, supporting your
hand on the mahlstick. Try to make your
movements as fluid as possible.

#### 6

Add the bunches of grapes, above and below
the stems using the round-ended brush.
Overlap the double lines in some places:
remember that you are aiming for a hand-
painted look, not a regular-repeat pattern.

# Foam-block Painting

*Printing with cut-out foam blocks must be the easiest possible way to achieve the effect of hand-blocked wallpaper, and it gives an irregularity of pattern that is impossible in machine-produced papers. Another special feature of this project is the paint that we have used – a combination of wallpaper paste, PVA glue and gouache colour. This is not only cheap, but it also has a wonderful translucent quality all of its own. The combination of sponge and paint works well, because pressing and lifting the sponge emphasizes the texture that results from using a slightly sticky paint.*

The best foam for cutting is high in density but still soft, such as upholsterer's foam; it needs to be at least 2.5 cm / 1 in thick. You need to be able to hold the foam firmly without distorting the printing surface.

Paint some of your background colour on to sheets of scrap paper, and then use this to try out your sponge-printing; use different densities and combinations of colour, making a note of the proportions of colour to paste in each one. This

means you will be able to mix up the same colour in a larger amount when you print on the wall (although the paint will go a very long way). The background used here is painted using the brushed-out colour glaze described on page 16.

## MATERIALS

*tracing paper, if necessary
upholsterer's foam off-cuts
felt-tipped pen
scalpel or craft knife
plumb-line
paper square measuring
15 × 15 cm / 6 × 6 in, or
according to your chosen spacing
wallpaper paste
PVA glue
gouache paint or ready-mixed
watercolour paint in viridian,
deep green and off-white
saucer
clear matt varnish (optional)*

**1**

Photocopy or trace the design from the template section and cut out the shapes to leave a stencil. Trace the design on to the foam and outline it using a felt-tipped pen.

**2**

Cut out the shapes using a sharp scalpel or craft knife: first cut around the pattern, and then part the foam slightly and cut through the entire thickness.

**3**

Attach the plumb-line to the wall/ceiling join in one corner. Now turn the square sheet of paper on the diagonal and let the plumb-line fall through the centre, lining up the top and bottom corners with the line. Make pencil dots on the wall at each corner. Move the square down the line, marking the corner points each time. Then move the line along sideways. Continue until the whole wall is marked with a grid of dots.

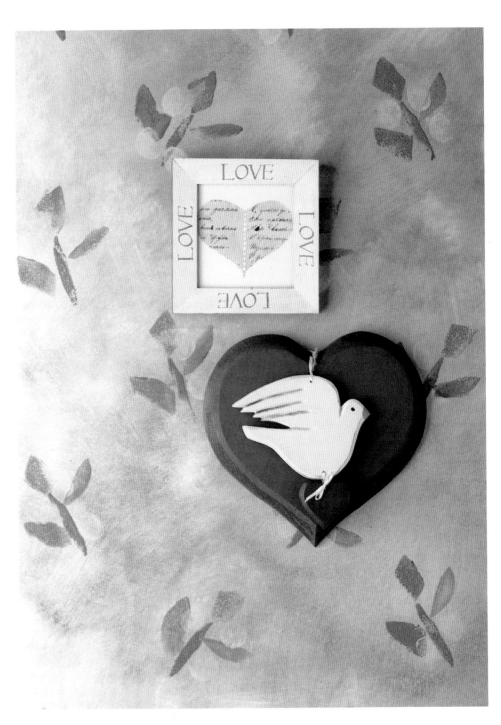

#### 4

Mix wallpaper paste and water according to the manufacturer's instructions. Add PVA glue, in the proportion 3 parts paste to 1 part PVA. Add a squeeze of viridian and deep green gouache paint or ready-mixed watercolour, and blend the ingredients until well mixed. Test the mixture on scrap paper, adding more colour if necessary.

#### 5

Put some paint into a saucer and dip the first sponge into it. Wipe off excess paint, and then print with the sponge using a light rolling motion. Lift and print again, using the pencil dots as a positioning guide.

#### 6

Use the second sponge to complete the sprig design with leaf shapes, varying the position slightly to add life.

#### 7

Use the dot-shaped sponge and the off-white colour to complete the motif with berries, adding the colour to the PVA mixture as before. Go over the leaves or stalks on some sprigs and let others 'float' alongside. If your walls are to be exposed to steam or splashes, or even fingerprints, you may like to protect this finish with a coat of clear matt varnish.

# 'Limed' Floorboards

*Liming sanded wooden floorboards gives a much softer impression than stains or tinted varnishes, reminiscent of scrubbed pine kitchen-tables, washed-out wooden spoons, or driftwood bleached by the sun and the sea. If you are lucky enough to possess a sandable floor, try this easy alternative to time-consuming conventional liming. The floor can be a traditional off-white, or tinted to any pastel shade.*

Raking-out the grain with a wire brush makes the channels for the paint, as well as clearing out any residual polish or varnish. If you like the wood grain to show as much as possible, wipe the surface with a damp cloth before it dries; the colour will then be concentrated in the raked-out grain of the floorboards. When the floor is dry, a coat of acrylic floor varnish will seal the colour.

MATERIALS

*coarse wire brush*
*white emulsion paint*
*acrylic paint in raw umber*
*large decorator's brush*
*clean damp cloth*
*clear matt varnish*

**1**

Use a wire brush to rake-out the wood following the grain direction at all times. Brush and vacuum the floor very carefully.

**2**

Mix up the wash, using 3 parts of water to 1 part of emulsion. Tint the colour with raw umber acrylic, or, if you prefer, use a pastel colour: pink, blue, green or yellow will all look good in the right setting, and very little of the actual colour will show. Experiment on spare boards.

**3**

Apply the wash with the decorator's brush, beginning in a corner at the skirting board and following the direction of the grain to the other edge.

**4**

Use a damp cloth to wipe away any excess paint and reveal the grain. A wet cloth will just wash away the paint, so keep it just damp for this. When the floor is completely dry, apply several coats of varnish to protect and seal the surface, allowing plenty of drying time between each coat.

# Hardboard Floor with Trompe-l'œil Dhurrie

*It is a sad fact that not every home is blessed with handsome floorboards, to be sanded and waxed to a golden gleam. Most older houses have a mixture of new and old boards that aren't good enough to be made into a feature.*

Hardboard can be a surprisingly attractive solution if you're faced with a low budget and a patchy selection of floorboards. The utilitarian appearance of hardboard means it is most often used as a levelling surface below vinyl; used in its own right, however, and decorated with stencils, it can look very stylish.

To counteract the potential drabness of a large area of hardboard this project shows how to paint a trompe-l'œil dhurrie in the centre of the room, so that the plain board becomes the border for the dhurrie. Hardboard provides a wonderfully smooth surface for painting and the dhurrie will provide a focal point that is guaranteed to be a talking point as well!

### MATERIALS

*newspaper*
*hardboard to fit the floor area*
*small hammer*
*panel pins*
*Stanley knife*
*ruler*
*tape measure*
*Crown Compatibles emulsion paint in shades 'Dusky Blue', 'Splash Blue' and 'Regency Cream'*
*2.5 cm / 1 in square-ended brush*
*acrylic paint in dark blue and black*
*decorator's brushes*
*masking tape*
*stencil card or Mylar*
*scalpel or craft knife*
*2 cm / ½ in stencil brush*
*clear matt varnish*

1

Lay sheets of newspaper on the floor to make an even surface. Fit the first sheet of hardboard into the corner nearest the door. Hammer in panel pins 7.5 cm / 3 in apart and 1.5 cm / ⅝ in in from the edge and fasten the hardboard to the existing floor.

2

Lay the next sheet of hardboard alongside the first, butting it hard up against the first sheet, and right up to the skirting board. Continue laying the whole boards across the room until you reach the point at which the hardboard needs to be trimmed to fit. Measure the space, at least twice, if it is not too large or awkwardly shaped; if it is irregularly shaped, make a newsprint pattern to be sure of getting a good fit. Cut the hardboard using a Stanley knife and a ruler on the shiny side, then breaking along the cut.

3

If you decide to place your dhurrie in the centre of the room, use a tape measure to find the centre line, and then measure out from it. The dhurrie can be as large or small as you like; this rug is made up of units 150 × 75 cm / 5 × 2½ feet, which you can multiply or divide to suit your room size. Mark the outline of the dhurrie on the floor. Outline the area with the square-ended brush and then fill in the Dusky Blue colour. Leave to dry for 2 hours.

4

Tint the blue to a darker shade by adding a squeeze of black acrylic, and then paint over the area with a dryish brush, to give the dhurrie a woven texture.

. . . continued

<u>5</u>

Trace and cut out the stencil design from the template section. Mask off the outer patterns with tape. Position the stencil 2 cm / ¾ in from the edge, and stencil the central design in Splash Blue emulsion. Remove the tape and clean the stencil.

<u>6</u>

Now mask off the central pattern and stencil the pattern on either side in Regency Cream emulsion.

<u>7</u>

Position the medallion stencil along the edge of the border and paint all the pattern, except for the outermost lines, in dark blue acrylic. You can mask off these lines with tape, as in the previous steps.

<u>8</u>

Mask off the central medallion and stencil the outer lines cream.

<u>9</u>

Soften the dark blue of the central medallions with light dabs of Splash Blue emulsion.

<u>10</u>

Apply at least two coats of clear varnish to the whole area.

# Cork-tile Chequer-board Floor

*Cork is a wonderful natural material that provides a warm, quiet and relatively cheap floor-covering. It has been largely confined to the kitchen and bathroom in the past, but should not be overlooked when choosing a floor for living areas.*

It is important to lay cork tiles on an even surface, so tack a layer of hardboard across the floorboards first. Use only floor-grade cork tiles. The unsealed tiles used here absorbed the coloured varnish well; two coats of clear polyurethane varnish with a satin finish gave a protective seal. You may prefer a proprietary brand of cork tile sealant.

### MATERIALS

*cork floor tiles*
*wood-stains in shades 'Dark Jacobean Oak' and 'Antique Pine'*
*large decorator's brush*
*cork-tile adhesive, if necessary*
*clear satin varnish*

## 1

Paint half of the tiles with the Dark Jacobean Oak wood-stain and the remaining tiles with the Antique Pine wood-stain and leave them to dry overnight. Measure the floor length to establish the number of Jacobean Oak tiles needed and cut half that number in half diagonally. Begin laying tiles in the corner that will be seen most; then, if you have to trim a tile at the other end, it will not be so obvious. If you are using self-adhesive tiles, simply peel off the backing.

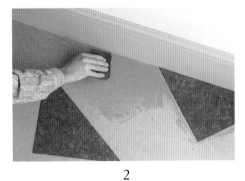

## 2

Lay the contrasting tiles next, tight up against the first row, wiping off any excess adhesive that has been forced up between the tiles, if you're using adhesive. Once you have laid the two rows, measure the nearest adjoining wall and cut half-tiles to fit the length of that skirting as well. Stick these down.

## 3

Now, work to fill the floor space diagonally. Trim the tiles at the opposite edge to fit snugly against the skirting board. Apply two coats of clear varnish to seal the floor. It is important to make sure that the first coat is bone-dry before you apply the next one, so be patient, and let it dry overnight.

# Acorn and Oak-leaf Border

*A painted border can offset the austerity of plain wooden floorboards, while the pattern links different areas without dominating the room. The scale of the oak-leaf pattern can be adjusted to suit the size of your room, but try to 'think big' and enlarge the design to at least four times larger than life size, otherwise the impact will be lost.*

Acorns and oak leaves have been used to decorate homes for hundreds of years, and they have a special place in country decorating. William Morris, the famous designer of the Arts and Crafts movement, used many country trees and plants in his patterns, and designed a wonderful wallpaper called 'Acorns'. Let the old saying 'Tall oaks from little acorns grow' be your inspiration, and use this painted-floor border as the basis for a warm and welcoming country-style living room.

Paint the background a dark colour and use paint with a matt finish as this will 'hold' your outline drawings better than a smooth or glossy paint. Begin at the corners and work towards the middle, using the templates as a measuring guide to work out your spacing. Once you have planned the placing of your design, work on a 60 cm / 24 in area at a time, using your whole arm to make the curves, not just the wrist. This way your painting will flow in a more natural way.

## MATERIALS

*medium-weight card*
*spray adhesive*
*scalpel or craft knife*
*masking tape*
*ruler*
*set square*
*National Trust paint in shade*
*'Off Black'*
*decorator's brush*
*white chinagraph pencil or chalk*
*white plate*
*gouache paint in yellow, sienna, umber, etc.*
*soft artist's brush*
*plank or long ruler*
*lining brush*
*clear matt varnish*

1

Use a photocopier to enlarge the oak-leaf and acorn pattern from the template section to at least four times life size (larger if you have a big room). Stick the enlargement on to medium-weight card and cut around the shape with scalpel or craft knife, to leave a cardboard template. Use masking tape, with a ruler and set square to outline the dark background colour. Apply the colour using the decorator's brush and leave to dry.

2

Beginning at the corner, draw around the oak-leaf template with the chinagraph pencil or chalk. Add stems or acorns to make the pattern fit around the corner, and then continue along the border. Use the template as a measuring guide, to make sure that the design fits comfortably.

3

Using a white plate as a palette, squeeze out several different tones of yellow, sienna, umber, etc. Mix them as you paint; this adds variety.

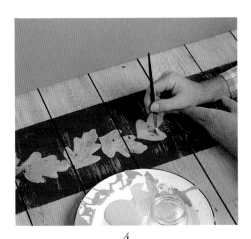

###### 4

Fill in the oak-leaf shapes, using subtle variations in colour for added interest.

###### 5

Add the finishing touches and flourishes like the leaf veining, stems and acorns.

###### 6

Use a straight edge, such as a plank, and a lining brush to paint the lines that enclose the border about 2.5 cm / 1 in from the edge. Apply 3–4 coats of clear varnish, allowing generous drying time (overnight if possible) between coats.

# Painted Canvas Floorcloth

*Canvas floorcloths were first used by the early American settlers, who had travelled across the sea from Europe. They recycled canvas sailcloth, painting it to imitate the oriental carpets that were popular with the rich merchants and aristocrats in their native lands. Many layers of linseed oil were applied to the painted canvas to make them waterproof and hard-wearing.*

The floorcloths were superseded by linoleum, and, unfortunately, few good old examples remain; they had no intrinsic value and were discarded when worn. Recently, however, they have undergone something of a revival. With the tough modern varnishes now available, they provide an unusual and hard-wearing alternative to the ubiquitous oriental rug.

The design for this floorcloth is based on a nineteenth-century quilt pattern called 'Sun, Moon and Stars'. The original quilt was made in very bright primary colours, but more muted shades work well for the floorcloth.

## MATERIALS

*craft knife or pair of sharp scissors
heavy artist's canvas (to order
from art supply shops)
pencil
ruler
strong fabric adhesive
drawing pin and 1 m / 1 yd length
of string
cardboard
acrylic paints in red, blue
and green
medium-size square-ended artist's
brush
medium-sized pointed artist's
brush
varnish in shade 'Antique Pine'
household paintbrush
medium-grade sandpaper*

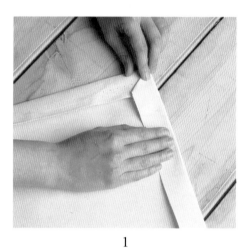

### 1

Cut the canvas to the size required, allowing an extra 4 cm / 1½ in all around. Draw a 4 cm / 1½ in wide border around the edge of the canvas and mitre the corners. Apply fabric adhesive to the border and fold it flat.

### 2

Referring to the diagram in the template section, find the centre-point of the canvas and secure the string to the drawing pin at this point. You will now be able to draw the five circles needed for the design, by holding a pencil at various distances along the length of the tautly pulled string. Keep the tension on the string to draw a perfect circle.

### 3

Cut three differently sized cardboard triangles to make the saw-toothed edges of the two circles and the outside border. Just move the triangle along the pencil guidelines using the card as a template to draw around.

### 4

Cut a card circle to make a template for the full moons and draw them in position. Then trim the circle to make the crescent and then the sickle moons, drawing them in position. Do the same for the stars.

### 5

Now start filling in the red. Use the flat-ended brush for larger areas and the pointed brush for outlines and fine work.

### 6

Fill in the pale blue and green circles of colour.

### 7

Apply 3–4 coats of Antique Pine varnish with a clean household brush, rubbing down each dried coat with sandpaper before applying the next one. Overnight drying is best.

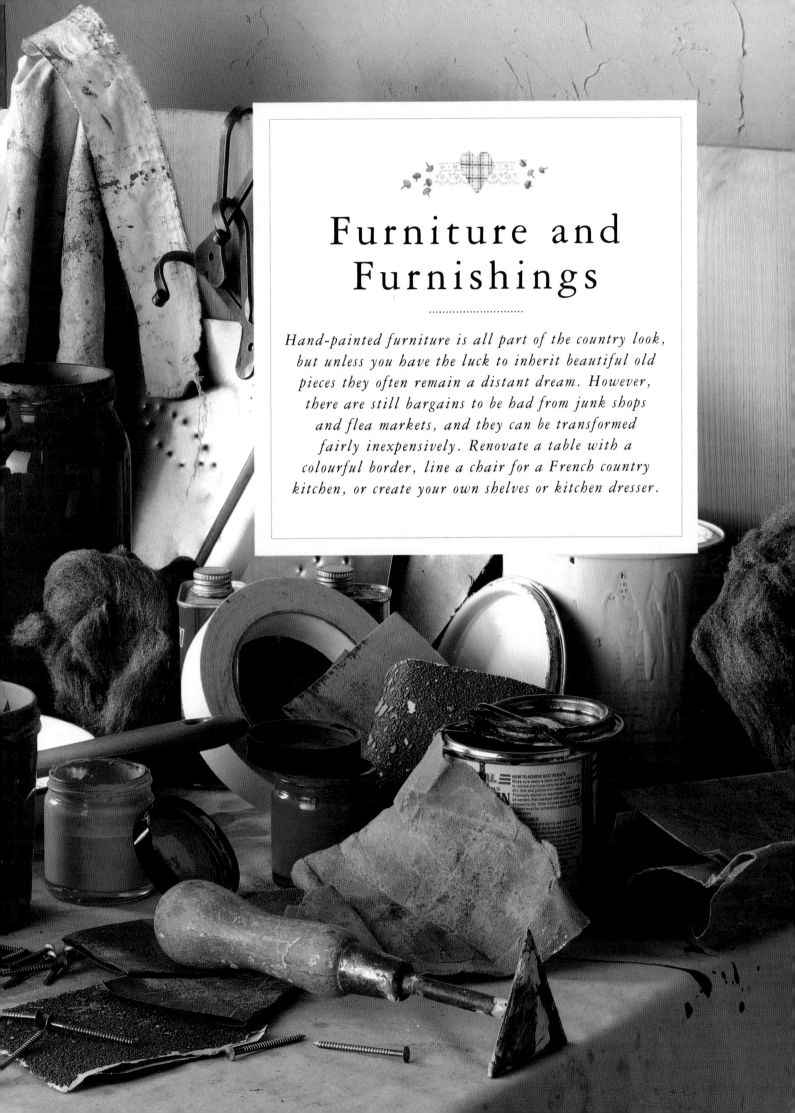

# Furniture and Furnishings

................................................

*Hand-painted furniture is all part of the country look, but unless you have the luck to inherit beautiful old pieces they often remain a distant dream. However, there are still bargains to be had from junk shops and flea markets, and they can be transformed fairly inexpensively. Renovate a table with a colourful border, line a chair for a French country kitchen, or create your own shelves or kitchen dresser.*

# Country-style Motifs and Patterns

There are three main sources of motifs in country style – nature, local tradition and religion. Nature and the elements are the strongest influences of all and are celebrated in the decoration of rural homes throughout the world. Flowers and foliage vary according to climate; this is reflected in patterns and motifs, although some plants, like the vine for instance, have been used decoratively since classical times and are found in the art of many cultures.

Many fruit, flower and foliage motifs have symbolic meanings too, and these were incorporated into homes for their protective value in warding off evil, or for the bringing of good fortune. The rose is used as a symbol of love, both divine and earthly, and the tulip stands for prosperity. The oak leaf and acorn are associated with great potential and the future, while ivy symbolizes tenacity. The sunflower radiates warmth and is guaranteed to bring thoughts of summer to winter days.

Animals, birds and fish feature as well. Wild creatures, farm animals, faithful pets and feathered friends all find their way into country crafts and patterns. The rooster has been used since early Christian times as a symbol of faith, but it is more likely to feature in country

ABOVE: *The tulip is a popular folk motif, and symbolizes prosperity.*

decorating in celebration of his great decorative shape, coupled with his early-morning tyranny.

Cats and dogs are often commemorated in embroideries or paintings, as are horses and other farmyard friends. Patchwork quilts feature many animal and fruit designs that have been stylized to great effect, and this, in turn, has created a style of stencilling whose origins are the quilt-maker's patterns rather than the original inspiration.

Religious influences are especially noticeable in Roman Catholic countries, where there is more emphasis on the visual celebration of faith. Shrines, altars, festive decorations and votive offerings are all a part of the decoration of rural homes in countries like Mexico, Spain, Italy and France.

Harvest motifs, like the wheat sheaf or the cornucopia are popular in most cultures. Fruits have been incorporated into woven and printed textiles, and vegetables are a favourite subject in 'theorem' paintings, a style of stencil paintings used in American folk art.

One of the most common country motifs is the heart: whether punched out of tin, carved out of planks or stencilled on to walls, the heart is everywhere. It symbolizes love and it is a uniquely simple and adaptable motif. The shape hardly changes at all, yet it can be used in many different ways without diminishing its effect. The heart has been used for many centuries across many cultures, and yet there still seems to be an infinite number of new ways to use it.

Geometric shapes have been borrowed from patchwork quilts, and suns, moons and stars will always be popular motifs. They are universal.

The beauty of country-style decorating is the nonchalance with which motifs, styles and patterns can be mixed. The only decorative effect to be avoided is mass-produced adulterated versions of country-style designs, because they will have lost their heart and soul in the manufacturing process!

LEFT: *Decorative surface detail is characteristic of country style, as in this free-hand painted box.*

RIGHT: *The heart, a perennial favourite, is appliquéd in a repeat pattern on this patchwork piece.*

CLOCKWISE FROM TOP LEFT: *Stencilled details give this chair a look of pure country. Geometric patterns are always popular choices for textiles. The free-hand, organic design on this box is inspired by nature. A tin heart is decorated with punched geometric patterns.*

# Painted Table

*It is still possible, thank goodness, to find bargain tables in junk shops, and this one cost less than a tenth of the price of a new one. It is the sort of table that you can imagine standing in a country cottage parlour, covered with a lace-edged cloth and laden with tea-time treats. There is no guarantee that you will find a similar table, but any old table could be decorated in the same way.*

Before you decorate your bargain, you may have to strip off the old paint or varnish and treat it for wood-worm, as we did. Any serious holes can be filled with wood-filler and then sanded and stained to match. The trick is to emphasize the good features and play down the bad. Old table-tops look more interesting than new ones and are well worth sanding, bleaching and staining. The stain on the table legs contrasts well with the red and green paint used on the table-top. The lining can be attempted free-hand, but masking tape makes the job much easier. Mark the position lightly in pencil so that all the lines are the same distance from the edge.

## MATERIALS

*table*
*wood-stain in shade 'Dark Jacobean Oak'*
*household paintbrush*
*emulsion paint in red and green*
*1 cm / ½ in square-ended artist's brush*
*masking tape*
*shellac*
*beeswax polish*
*soft clean cloth*

**1**

Prepare and treat the table as necessary. Use a rag to rub the wood-stain into the table legs, applying more as it is absorbed into the wood. The finish should be an even, almost black tone.

**2**

Paint the base of the table-top with red emulsion.

**3**

Measure 5 cm / 2 in in from the edge of the table and place a strip of masking tape this distance in from each of the edges. Leave a 2 cm / ¾ in gap and then place the next strips of tape to run parallel with the first set.

**4**

Fill in the strip between the tape with the green paint and leave to dry.

<u>5</u>

Apply two coats of shellac to the table.

<u>6</u>

Finish the table with a coat of beeswax polish, buffing it to a warm sheen with a soft clean cloth.

# Painted Chest

*Before the eighteenth century, throughout northern Europe and Scandinavia a country bride took her own decorated linen chest into her new home. The dowry chest would have been made by her father, lovingly carved and painted as a farewell gift to his daughter. Marriage customs accounted for many rural crafts, and the family took great pride in providing a handsome chest for a bride. This custom was continued among the first settlers in North America.*

The chest used in this project is a mixture of Old- and New-World influences. The shape is English, but the painted decoration was inspired by an old American dowry chest. The pattern used on the chest is geometric, but the paint finish is very loosely applied, to give a good contrast between two styles. You can use the pattern to decorate any blanket chest, old or new, and then give it an antique finish with tinted varnish.

The most time-consuming aspect is the accurate drawing-up of the pattern shapes, but it is worth spending time to get the proportions right. The combing and spotting has to be done quickly, so the effect is one of controlled chaos!

### MATERIALS

*blanket chest
shellac, if necessary
Crown Compatibles paint in shades 'Dusky Blue' and 'Regency Cream'
household paintbrushes
tracing paper
pair of compasses
ruler
acrylic varnish in shade 'Antique Pine'
graining comb
clean damp cloth*

1

If you are starting with bare wood, apply a coat of shellac to seal the surface.

2

Paint the chest with Dusky Blue emulsion. Trace and enlarge the pattern from the template section and use it as a guide to position the panels. Draw the panels with a pair of compasses and ruler.

3

Fill in all the panels with cream emulsion.

4

Apply a thick coat of varnish to one panel only.

### 5

Quickly comb the varnish in a pattern,
following the shape of the panel. Make one
smooth combing movement into the wet
varnish, and then wipe the comb to prevent
any build-up of varnish. Complete one panel
before repeating steps 4 and 5 for the others.

### 6

Apply a coat of varnish to the whole chest.
Immediately take a just-damp cloth,
screw it into a ball and use it to dab off spots
of the varnish.

# Painted Bench

*Every home should have a bench like this, to squeeze extra guests around the dinner table and to keep by the back door for comfortable boot-changing. This bench was made by a carpenter, from a photograph seen in a book of old country furniture. The wood is reclaimed floorboards, which give just the right rustic feel to the bench.*

The decoration is applied in a rough folk-art style that adds a touch of humour. You can use this style to decorate any bench, and even a plain modern design will lose its hard edges and take on the character of a piece of rustic hand-made furniture.

MATERIALS

*bench*
*medium-grade sandpaper*
*shellac*
*household paintbrushes*
*emulsion paint in deep red,*
*dark blue-grey and light blue-green*
*small piece of sponge*
*varnish in shade 'Antique Pine'*
*clear matt varnish*

### 1

Sand the bare wood and seal it with a coat of shellac.

### 2

Paint the legs in dark blue-grey emulsion, working directly on to the wood.

### 3

Paint the seat with the deep red emulsion.

### 4

Use the sponge to dab an even pattern of blue-green spots across the whole surface of the seat.

### 5

When the paint is dry, rub the seat and edges with sandpaper, to simulate the wear and tear of a thousand harvest suppers.

### 6

Apply one coat of Antique Pine varnish to the whole bench. Then apply two more coats of matt varnish for a strong finish.

# Shaker-inspired Peg Rail

*The Shakers were a religious movement whose ideals inspired a style of furnishings and furniture of great simplicity and beauty of form. They did not believe in ornamentation or decoration for its own sake, but held that functional objects should be as beautiful and as well made as possible. The name 'Shaker' comes from the ecstatic movements that occurred in their worship.*

Peg rails were very characteristic of Shaker homes, and were used for hanging all kinds of utensils and even chairs, keeping the floor clear. Our rail is a very inexpensive and simplified version of the Shaker idea, and what it lacks in fine craftsmanship it makes up for in practicality. We have used a pine plank, with a sawn-up broom-handle to make the pegs. These rails work well all around the house, but are especially useful in hallways, children's rooms and bathrooms. The coat of paint is not strictly Shaker in style, but will disguise the rail's humble origins.

## MATERIALS

pine plank 2.5 cm / 1 in thick
ruler
saw
plane
drill with bit for broom-handle holes
1 or 2 broom-handles
medium-grade sandpaper
wood glue
wooden block and hammer
shellac
household paintbrushes
Crown Compatibles emulsion paint in shade 'Dusky Blue'
varnish in shade 'Antique Pine'
white spirit, if necessary
spirit-level
rawl plugs and long screws

**1**
Measure and cut the wood to the length required. Plane it to smooth and round the edges.

**2**
Mark the peg positions 20 cm / 8 in apart along the length. The spacing can be altered to suit your requirements.

**3**
Drill holes 1.5 cm / ⅝ in deep in which to recess the pegs.

**4**
Cut up the broom-handles into 13 cm / 5 in lengths. Sand the edges to round them off.

<u>5</u>

Apply wood glue and fit the pegs into their holes using a small wooden block and hammer to fit them securely.

<u>6</u>

Apply one coat of shellac to seal the surface of the wood.

<u>7</u>

Paint the rail blue.

<u>8</u>

Use medium-grade sandpaper to rub back to bare wood along the edges.

<u>9</u>

Give the whole shelf a coat of Antique Pine varnish. Dip a rag in white spirit (for polyurethane varnish) or water (for acrylic varnish) and rub off some of the varnish. Use a spirit-level and ruler to mark the position of the rail on the wall. Drill holes through the rail at 40 cm / 18 in intervals. Drill into the wall, using suitable wall-fixings and screws.

# Painted and Lined Country Chair

*It is always worth buying interesting individual chairs when you spot them, as they are often very inexpensive if they need 'doing up'. Four mismatching chairs painted the same way will make a convincing and charming set, and the effect is pure country.*

This is a typical French, country-style, rush-seated chair, with curvaceous lines just begging to be accentuated with lining. The essentials of sturdiness and comfort have not been ignored, the seat is generously woven and it is very comfortable. (It is always worth sitting on your chair before you buy because it may have been custom-made for a differently shaped person!)

Colour is a real revitalizer and we have chosen a yellow and blue colour scheme reminiscent of the painter Monet's kitchen, to bring out the French character of the chair. It is worth spending time preparing the wood, and this may mean stripping all the paint if there are several layers of gloss. If you do have the chair professionally stripped, the joints will need to be re-glued, because the caustic stripper dissolves glue as well as paint.

## MATERIALS

*country-style chair*
*medium-grade sandpaper*
*undercoat*
*household paintbrushes*
*shellac and wood primer,*
*if necessary*
*Crown Satinwood paint in yellow*
*wire wool*
*hard pencil*
*tube of artist's oil colour in*
*ultramarine blue*
*white spirit*
*long-haired square-ended*
*artist's brush*
*varnish in shade 'Antique Pine'*

### 1

If the chair hasn't been stripped, rub it down well with medium-grade sandpaper. Apply the undercoat, or if the chair has been stripped, give it a coat of shellac followed by wood primer. Paint the chair yellow.

### 2

When this coat has dried, use wire wool to rub the paint back along the edges where natural wearing away would take place. With a pencil draw the lining, following the curves of the chair.

### 3

Mix the oil paint with white spirit in the proportions 3 parts paint to 1 part white spirit. You need paint that flows smoothly from the brush and allows you to retain control. If you find the paint too runny, add more colour. Practise the brushstroke with the artist's brush on scrap paper or board, supporting your brush-hand with your spare hand. Controlling your lines is a matter of confidence, which grows as you paint. Paint the lining on the legs, chairback and seat.

### 4

When dry, rub back with wire wool in places, as you did with the yellow.

### 5

Finally apply a coat or two of varnish to soften the colour and protect the lining.

# Pie-safe Cupboard

*Cupboards like this one were mainly used in America as cooling cupboards for freshly baked goods. The doors were made out of decoratively punched and pierced tin sheets that allowed the delicious aromas to waft out, but prevented flies from getting in. They were called 'safes' because they were fitted with locks to keep temptation out of reach of little fingers lured by delicious smells!*

We used an existing old pine cupboard to make the pie-safe, replacing the wooden front panels with newly pierced tin ones. Milled-steel sheet can be bought from sheet-metal suppliers, or try asking at a hardware store or looking in Yellow Pages. Care must be taken, as the edges of the sheet are very sharp, and need to be folded over to make a safe seam. You can crimp or flatten the edges using pliers.

The actual patterning is done with a hammer and nail, or, for more linear piercing, you can use a small chisel. This pattern is our own interpretation of a traditional design, but once you begin, your own style will emerge. You may find other ways of making patterns, perhaps using the end of a Phillips screwdriver, for instance – really anything goes. If the cupboard is to be used in the kitchen, add a protective backing sheet behind the tin, to cover the sharp edges. To get rid of the very new gleam of pierced metal, rub vinegar into the surface.

## MATERIALS

*old cupboard with one or two panelled doors*
*tracing paper*
*medium-grade sandpaper*
*shellac, if necessary*
*24- or 26-gauge milled-steel sheet(s) to fit (allow 1 cm / ½ in all around for the seams)*
*pliers and tinsnips, if necessary*
*masking tape*
*pair of compasses or transfer paper*
*chinagraph pencil*
*hammer*
*selection of different nails, screwdrivers and chisels*
*backing material such as hardboard, if necessary*
*panel pins*
*varnish in shade 'Antique Pine'*
*household paintbrush*

### 1

Remove any beading and ease out the existing panels from the cupboard doors. Measure the space and use tracing paper to plan the design to fit. Rub down the cupboard with sandpaper. If it has been stripped, re-seal it with a coat of shellac. Trim the metal sheet, if necessary. Fold over the sharp edge of the metal sheet, to make a seam about 1 cm / ½ in deep around the edge. Crimp firmly with pliers. Put masking tape over sharp edges, to prevent accidental cuts.

### 2

Transfer your design on to the tin surface, using a pair of compasses. If you find this tricky, trace the whole design and use transfer paper to put it on to the metal. Add any extra designs with the chinagraph pencil.

### 3

Practise piercing on a scrap of tin, such as a biscuit-tin lid, so that you know how hard you need to hit the nail to pierce a hole, and also how just to dent the surface without piercing it. Place thick cardboard or an old towel or blanket beneath the tin to absorb the noise and protect the surface underneath. Once you are confident with the hammer and nail, or whatever tool you want to use, hammer out the pattern.

### 4

Fit the pierced panels, and the backing if you are using it, into the door and replace the beading to secure it. Use short panel pins at a distance of 4 cm / 1½ in apart, all around the panel to fix in place.

### 5

Sandpaper the edges to simulate a time-worn effect. Give the wood a protective coat of antiquing varnish.

# Shelf with Hanging Hooks

*This large shelf with a backboard and hooks would suit a kitchen, entrance hall or large bathroom. It is really simple to make, requiring only the most basic of carpentry skills and tools. The shelf can be painted or varnished, depending on the wood, and it's a really handsome and useful piece of furniture.*

The very best wood to use is reclaimed pine, usually floorboards. Demolition or builder's reclamation yards usually have stocks of old wood, but be prepared to pay more for old than new pine. If you're leaving the shelf unpainted it's definitely worth the extra money for old wood. If you intend to paint the shelf, new wood can be used for the backing board, to cut down on the price.

The best feature of the shelf is the very generously sized brackets, which were copied from an old farm storeroom. They have been cut from a section of old pine door, using a jig-saw. The brackets will support the shelf and balance the weight, but the shelf should be screwed into a sound brick wall, using suitable rawl plugs and long steel screws.

This type of shelf is very popular in rural eastern European communities. The hooks can either be new brass or wrought-iron coathooks; or you may be lucky enough to find an old set. Either way they are bound to be concealed, as hooks usually attract more than they were ever intended to hold!

### MATERIALS

*tracing paper*
*piece of pine 34 cm × 18 cm × 3 cm / 14½ in × 7 in × 1¼ in thick, for the brackets*
*jig-saw*
*drill with No. 5 and 6 bits*
*pine plank 100 cm × 15 cm × 2 cm / 3 ft 4 in × 6 in × ¾ in thick, for the backboard*
*pine plank 130 cm × 22 cm × 2 cm / 4 ft 4 in × 8½ in × ¾ in thick, for the shelf*
*wood glue*
*wood-screws*
*shellac*
*household paintbrush*
*2.5 cm / 1 in brush*
*Crown Compatibles emulsion paint in shades 'Dusky Blue', 'Aqua Spring', and 'Precious Jade'*
*clean damp cloth*
*wire wool*
*medium-grade sandpaper*
*6 coathooks*
*rawl plugs, if necessary*
*3 long screws*

**1**

Trace the bracket pattern from the template section and enlarge it until the longest side measures 33.5 cm / 13½ in. Trace this on to the wood, fitting it into one corner, and then flip the pattern over and trace it again into the opposite-end corner. The two can be cut out at the same time, using a jig-saw. Use the number 5 drill bit to make two holes through the backboard into the brackets; and also through the shelf down into the brackets. Spread wood glue on all the joining edges, and then screw them together with wood-screws.

**2**

Apply one coat of shellac to the whole unit.

**3**

Use the 2.5 cm / 1 in brush to apply a coat of Dusky Blue emulsion.

4

When dry, apply a coat of Aqua Spring.

5

Immediately afterwards, use a damp cloth to
wipe the paint off in some areas.

6

Paint the edges of the shelf and brackets with
Precious Jade.

7

Rub away some of the dried paint using wire
wool. This will reveal the wood grain
along the edges.

8

Finally rub down with medium-grade
sandpaper to smooth the finish and reveal the
grain. Screw in the hooks. Attach to the wall
by drilling through the backboard to make
holes for long wood-screws. Use suitable
wall fixings, if necessary.

# Painted Dresser

*If there is one item of furniture that typifies country style in most people's minds, it must surely be the dresser. A sturdy base cupboard topped with china-laden shelves is an irresistible sight.*

This dresser was made by a local carpenter using reclaimed pine, but a dresser can easily be made up using a sturdy chest of drawers combined with a set of bookshelves. The trick is to make sure that the two are balanced visually, with the height and depth of the shelves suiting the width of the base. You can join the two unobtrusively by using strong steel brackets at the back, and painting will complete the illusion that the two were made for each other.

The washed-out paint finish is achieved by using no undercoat and rubbing the dried paint back to the wood with sandpaper and wire wool. Alternatively you can rub some areas of the wood with candle wax before you begin painting; the candle wax will resist the paint, leaving the wood bare.

MATERIALS

dresser, or combination of shelves
and base cupboard
shellac
household paintbrushes
Crown Compatibles emulsion
paint in shades 'Dusky Blue',

'Quarry-tile Red' (optional) and
'Regency Cream'
household candle (optional)
medium-grade sandpaper and
wire wool
varnish in shade 'Antique Pine'

1

Apply a coat of shellac to seal the bare wood.

2

Paint the dresser Dusky Blue, following the direction of the grain. Allow to dry.

3

If desired, rub candle wax along the edges of the dresser before painting with a second colour.

4

The wax will prevent the second colour from adhering completely, and will create a distressed effect. Add the second colour, if using.

52

### 5

Paint the backing boards Regency Cream, again following the direction of the grain.

### 6

When the paint has dried, use medium-grade sandpaper and wire wool to rub back to bare wood along the edges, to simulate wear and tear.

### 7

Finally apply a coat of Antique Pine varnish to the whole dresser to protect the surface.

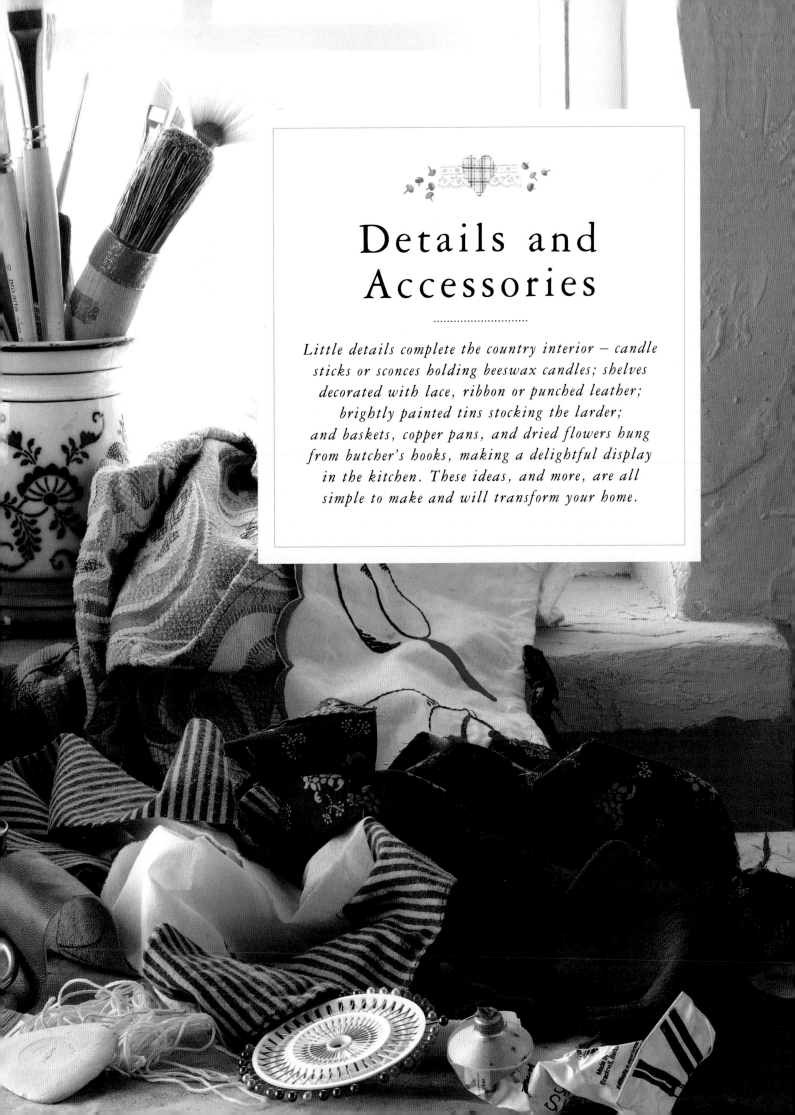

# Details and Accessories

*Little details complete the country interior – candle sticks or sconces holding beeswax candles; shelves decorated with lace, ribbon or punched leather; brightly painted tins stocking the larder; and baskets, copper pans, and dried flowers hung from butcher's hooks, making a delightful display in the kitchen. These ideas, and more, are all simple to make and will transform your home.*

# Finishing Touches

Once you have transformed your home with country-style paint finishes, furniture and flooring, it is time to add the finishing touches. The accumulation of 'finds' that add personality to a home does take time, and should be a gradual process; it often depends on your being in the right place at the right time. An unlimited supply of money would buy you folk-art treasures and an interior-designed country look, but you would certainly miss out on the pleasure of making your own accessories.

There are projects in this section to suit most talents and skills, whether your talent lies with a needle and thread, carpenter's tools or paintbrushes.

A simple broom-handle can be used to display a collection of baskets hanging from the ceiling and découpage transforms any ordinary tray into one to be displayed on the wall as 'art'.

Shelving can be dressed up with lace, ribbons, paper or even punched leather, to make something functional into a decorative feature. It is well worth seeking out a local carpenter if you lack

ABOVE: *This punched-tin sconce creates a wonderful backdrop for candles.*

the space or inclination to make your own shelving, because reclaimed timber like pine floorboarding is really worth using for its character and colour.

Candlelight is essential for adding a cosy atmosphere, and whether you choose to make the baluster candlesticks or the rustic wall sconce, you will be enriching the room with something unusual and hand-made. Use the ideas suggested as a starting point, adding your own colour schemes and patterns to give each thing you make a personal touch.

The embroidered pelmet looks very special, and the shapes do not require any particular needlecraft skill to follow. A simple chain stitch could be used to outline all the shapes, and satin stitch for the scallops. The more advanced embroiderer could elaborate upon the designs, filling the background as well as the kitchen implements with a variety of colours and fancy stitchwork.

Similarly, the patchwork throw does not need any more than basic sewing-machine skills to fit it together. The design will vary, depending on your selection of warm winter scarves and backing fabric, and the more experienced seamstress will be tempted to make the pattern more complicated by adding differently shaped patches. Whether you choose to make the basic throw or a more complicated variation, you are bound to be delighted with the result. It looks great draped over a chair and is marvellously warm and insulating on a cold country evening.

There are many country crafts that can be studied and mastered, like basket-making, weaving or the carving of decoy ducks. If you have time to explore and learn about how things are traditionally made, it is very enriching. Our projects are more about taking short cuts and making an impact, which is a good creative starting point. Once you realize the pleasure that is to be gained from both making and displaying your own creations, you are bound to continue to experiment and to enjoy country crafts.

LEFT AND RIGHT: *Beauty and practicality are the keynotes of any country kitchen. Utensils are displayed within easy reach, and dried goods may be kept in colourfully painted tins.*

CLOCKWISE FROM TOP LEFT: *A painted salt box, Shaker-style doll and varnished trug all add a feeling of country. Candles complete the scene. Sewing odds and ends can be kept tidy in a wooden box. These whirligigs form an eye-catching still-life with a collection of plates in complementary colours. A colour-washed tin lantern sets off a display of beeswax candles.*

# Wall Sconce

*These fashionable room accessories were once essential to every household; however, one wonders what our ancestors would make of us forsaking the convenience of electricity for the 'romance' of candlelight. The truth is that technology and mass-production seem to take the humanity out of our homes, making us long for the irregularity of candlelight, hand-stitching and country-crafted furniture.*

## MATERIALS

*old piece of wood*
*saw*
*hammer*
*brass and black upholstery tacks*
*wood glue*
*nails*

#### 1

Saw through the wood, making two sections to be joined at right angles. Begin the pattern by hammering the upholstery tacks in a central line; the pattern can then radiate from it.

#### 2

Form arrows, diamonds and crosses, using the contrast between the brass and black tacks to enhance your design.

#### 3

Apply a coating of wood glue to the sawn edge of the base. Hammer fine nails through the back into the base.

# Découpage Tray

*A good tray will be strong enough to carry the tea things and handsome enough to hang up as a decoration when not in use. This one has been découpaged with a selection of old engraving tools, but you could follow the method using any design you choose.*

Découpage takes you back to childhood; cutting out and gluing is a favourite activity of children between the ages of five and ten. The grown-up version is slightly more sophisticated, but the fun remains.

The secret of good découpage lies in accurate cutting and in putting on enough coats of varnish. Serious enthusiasts use 30 layers, rubbing back with fine sandpaper between the coats. The idea is to bring the background up to the level of the applied decoration, and then to add further depth with more coats, possibly to include crackle glaze and antique varnish. The final result should be convincing to both eye and touch.

## MATERIALS

*tray
Paint Magic woodwash in shade
'Maize'
household paintbrush
fine-grade sandpaper
photocopied motifs to cut out
sharp-pointed scissors or scalpel
wallpaper paste and brush
soft cloth
new paintbrush for varnishing
clear satin varnish
crackle glaze (optional)
artist's oil paint in raw umber*

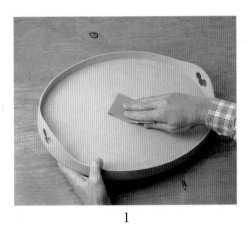

**1**

Prepare the tray by painting it with Maize as a base colour. When dry, rub the surface with fine-grade sandpaper.

**2**

Cut out your paper shapes carefully, moving the paper towards the scissors, or around on the cutting surface, so that you are always using the scissors or scalpel in the most comfortable and fluid way.

**3**

Turn the cut-outs over and paste the backs with wallpaper paste, right up to the edges, covering the whole area.

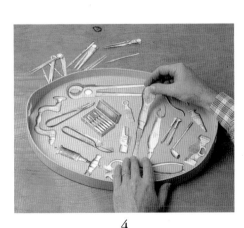

**4**

Stick them down in position on the tray.

. . . continued

DETAILS AND ACCESSORIES

### 5

Use a soft cloth to smooth out any bubbles.
Leave to dry overnight.

### 6

Begin varnishing, using a clean new brush
and applying a sparing coat to the whole
surface of the tray. When dry, rub lightly
with fine-grade sandpaper and repeat as many
times as possible.

### 7

A further dimension has been added to this
découpage, by the application of a crackle
glaze. There are several brands on the
market. It is best to follow the specific
instructions for the product you use.
Here the base varnish is being painted
on to the tray

### 8

When this coat is dry (after 20 minutes),
apply an even coat of crackle glaze and leave
it to dry for 20 minutes.

### 9

Rub a small amount of artist's oil paint into
the cracks, using a cotton cloth. Raw umber
was used here, which gives a naturally aged
effect but any colour can be used.

### 10

When the cracks have been coloured,
gently rub the excess paint from the surface,
using a soft cloth.

### 11

Give the tray at least two more coats of clear
satin varnish; many more if time and
patience allow.

# Wooden Candlesticks

*This pair of matching wooden candlesticks have been made from old balusters that were removed from a stair rail. This is an easy way to make something from turned wood without having to operate a lathe yourself. Balusters can be bought singly from wood merchants or DIY stores.*

The only special equipment needed is a vice and a flat-head drill bit, to make a hole in the top of the baluster large enough to hold a candle.

The candlesticks have been painted in bright earthy colours, giving a matching pair fit to grace any country table.

MATERIALS

*saw*
*2 wooden balusters (reclaimed or new)*
*2 square wood off-cuts*
*medium- and fine-grade sandpaper*
*wood glue*
*vice*

*electric drill fitted with a flat-head drill bit*
*acrylic paint in bright yellow, red and raw umber or burnt sienna*
*household and artist's brushes*
*clear matt acrylic varnish*
*soft clean cloth*

### 1

Cut out the most interesting section of the baluster and a square base; this one measures 7.5 × 7.5 cm / 3 × 3 in. Roughen the bottom of the baluster with sandpaper.

### 2

Very slightly, chamfer the base with fine-grade sandpaper. Glue the two sections together with wood glue.

### 3

Hold the candlestick securely in the vice and drill a hole for the candle 2 cm / ¾ in in diameter and 2 cm / ¾ in deep.

### 4

Paint with two or three coats of bright yellow acrylic paint.

### 5

Apply a coat of orange acrylic paint (add a touch of red to the yellow acrylic).

### 6

Tint the varnish to a muddy brown, by adding a squeeze of raw umber or burnt sienna. Brush this over the orange.

**7**

Use a crumpled cloth to lift some varnish and reveal the colour below.

63

# Woollen Patchwork Throw

*Believe it or not, this stunning chair throw cost next to nothing to make, and was finished in an afternoon! It is made from pure woollen scarves and remnant wool fabric. The scarves come from charity shops, and can be bought for pennies. You will be spoilt for choice, so choose a colour scheme derived from your remnant. The throw is lined with a length of old brocade curtain, but a flannel sheet would also be suitable, especially if you dyed it a dark colour.*

The only skill you need for this project is the ability to sew a straight line on a sewing machine: and tartan scarves provide good guidelines to follow. Clear a good space on the floor and lay the fabric and scarves out, moving them around until you are happy with the colour combinations. Cut out the first central square. The diamond shape will need to be hemmed and tacked before you sew it to the centre of the first square; after this, each strip of scarf will just need to be pinned and sewn in position.

The throw could easily be adapted to make a bedcover, and, because of the fine-quality wool used for scarves, it will be exceptionally warm. The challenge with this throw is to resist draping yourself in it, instead of the chair!

*scissors*
*about 1 m / 1 yd wool fabric*
*selection of plaid and plain*
*woollen scarves*
*pins, thread and sewing machine*
*old curtain or flannel sheet,*
*for lining*

**1**

Cut out a 46 × 46 cm / 18 × 18 in square of your 'background' fabric. Choose the pattern for your central diamond and cut a square, using the width of the scarf as the measurement for the sides. Turn the edges under 1 cm / ½ in and tack. Pin and sew the diamond in position.

**2**

Choose two scarves and cut them into four rectangles. Position them along the sides of the square, with the matching patterns facing each other. Sew them in place and trim off any excess.

**3**

Cut out four matching plain squares and pin and sew them into the corners. Check on the right side, to make sure that the corners meet accurately. Cut four strips of the background fabric to fit the sides.

**4**

Cut out four corner pieces of the scarf used for the central diamond, 14 cm × 14 cm / 5½ in × 5½ in. Sew a square to one end of each strip of background fabric.

**5**

Pin and then sew these long strips in position around the edge of the patchwork.

**6**

Cut a plain scarf into four strips lengthways and sew these around the outside edge, overlapping at the corners to complete the square.

**7**

Cut the lining to fit and sew the two pieces together, with their right sides facing inwards.

**8**

Turn inside out and sew up the seam by hand. Press, using a damp cloth and dry iron.

# Plaited 'Rag-rug' Tie-backs

*Tie-backs are an attractive way of getting the maximum amount of daylight into the house. It is surprising how much difference a few inches more exposure of window panes can make to the light in a room, so unless your windows are huge, it is well worth tying your curtains back into the wall. This idea has a real hands-on feel and can be made to co-ordinate or contrast with existing curtains.*

This method of plaiting scraps of fabric has been stolen from rag-rug makers, and if you have always wanted to make one, this may be just the introduction that you need! If you have any fabric left over from your curtains, you could incorporate this into the plaits. If not, one plain colour that appears in your curtaining will have a harmonizing effect on the whole scheme.

### MATERIALS

*scraps of fabric cut into 7.5-cm /
3-in wide strips
safety pin
needle and thread
scissors
strip of fabric for backing (one for
each tie-back)
2 D-rings for each tie-back*

**1**

Roll up the fabric strips, leaving a workable length unfurled.

**2**

Join three strips together, rolling one fabric around the other two and pinning them together with the safety pin. Attach the ends to a chair or any suitable stationary object or anchor them under a heavy weight. Begin plaiting, rolling the strips into tubes as you go, so that the rough edges are turned in and concealed. Make tight plaits. The tie-back needs to be at least 50 cm / 20 in long and four plaits deep.

**3**

Work until you have the required length and number of plaits. Lay the plaits flat and sew the edges together using a large needle and strong thread pulled up tight. Keep the plaits flat when you turn at either end.

**4**

Cut a backing strip, allowing enough fabric to turn under 1.5 cm / ⅝ in all round. Attach the D-rings at either end as you slip-stitch the lining into place.

# Quilted Tie-backs

*This is a quilting project for the absolute beginner. All that is required is the ability to sew an even running stitch along a drawn line. The pattern is a standard quilting stencil (available from craft shops), which you draw through using a chalky coloured pencil. A layer of wadding is placed between two strips of fabric, which can then be tacked or pinned together.*

The effect produced by the quilting is textural and the pattern shows up very well. The quilting is best done on plain fabrics, like the calico we used, but the tie-backs could be used with patterned curtains. Gingham or larger checked patterns look especially good teamed with quilted calico.

### MATERIALS

*1 m / 1 yd unbleached calico
scissors
50 cm / 20 in quilter's
wadding
quilt stencil pattern
chalky coloured pencil
pins, needle and thread
2 D-rings for each tie-back*

1

Cut the calico into strips 50 cm × 14 cm / 20 in × 5¾ in. Cut the wadding into strips 48 cm × 10 cm / 19 in × 4 in. Use the stencil to draw on to one piece of calico. Put a layer of wadding in between two layers of calico and pin.

2

Sew a running stitch along the pattern lines. You may find it easiest to pull the needle through each time, rather than sewing in and out of all three layers at once.

3

When the pattern is complete, fold in the edges and stitch them all around, either by hand or machine. Attach a D-ring at each end.

# Leather-edged Shelf Trimming

*Not all shelves are worthy of display, especially the new and inexpensive ones that are readily available in DIY stores. There is no denying that they are practical and functional, and a simple shelf trimming will transform them very quickly into a charming and individual room feature.*

### MATERIALS

*leather off-cuts (sold by weight in craft shops)*
*round template with a 7.5 cm / 3 in diameter*
*pencil, ruler and chalk*
*pinking shears*
*multi-sized hole punch*
*double-sided tape or glue*

### 1

Cut strips of leather to fit the length of your shelf, using several sections to make up the length if necessary. The edging needs to be 6 cm / 2½ in deep. Draw a line 1 cm / ½ in from the edge (on the reverse side) and use the template to draw semi-circles along the length of the line.

### 2

Cut around these with pinking shears. Punch out holes around the edges, varying the sizes.

### 3

Draw stars on the semi-circles with chalk. Punch out holes around the star outlines in the same way. Run a strip of double-sided tape along the shelf, and use this to attach the leather trim; alternatively all-purpose glue can be used.

# Lace and Gingham Shelf Trimming

*The lacy look may not suit every room, but it can add a very French touch to a dresser or kitchen shelf. The contrast between stout enamel pans and fine cotton lace can be quite charming; in French country homes, crochet lace is pinned up for display on any shelf available.*

There are so many different lace designs available, that the decision will have to be a personal one. You may go for an antique hand-crocheted piece or a simpler machine-made design. The pointed edging chosen here suits a china display very well.

There is something both cheerful and practical about gingham. It is perfectly suited to edging food-cupboard shelves, where the pattern is strong enough to stand out against all the different packaging designs. The combination with lace is fresh and pretty.

MATERIALS:

*strips of lace the length of the cupboard shelves, plus extra for turnings*
*cold tea*
*small bowl*

*scissors*
*double-sided tape*
*gingham ribbon the length of the sides of the shelves*
*all-purpose glue*

1

To tone down the brightness of this new lace, it was dipped into a bowl of cold tea. The stronger the brew, the darker the colour, so adjust it by adding water to lighten the dye, if necessary. Press the lace when dry and cut it to the correct length.

2

Apply the double-sided tape to the vertical sides of the shelves and peel off the backing tape. Cut the gingham ribbon to fit and seal the ends with a little glue, which will dry clear and prevent the ends from fraying.

3

Stick the gingham ribbon to the verticals, carefully smoothing it out and keeping it straight. Start at one end, and keep the ribbon taut.

4

Apply double-sided tape to the edges of the shelves, overlapping the gingham.

5

Seal one end of the lace with a small amount of glue. Stretch it along the tape, cut it to fit and seal the edge. Repeat for the other shelves.

# French Bread Bin

*The kitchen and meal-times play a central role in country life, entailing warm winter suppers when the nights have drawn in, or long, languorous lunches in the height of summer. Crusty bread is an integral part of any meal, and this stylish bread bin will bring a touch of French country style to your kitchen. The same design could be used in a hallway or by the back door to hold umbrellas or walking sticks.*

The pattern provided in the template section could be given to a carpenter, or, if woodworking is a hobby, made at home. The stand has been made from reclaimed pine floorboards, which are quite heavy and give it stability, as does the moulding used to broaden the base.

The decoration is called ferning and was very popular in Victorian times. Dried or imitation ferns (florist's sell fake plastic or silk ones) are sprayed with aerosol mounting adhesive and arranged on the surface, which is then spray-painted. It dries very quickly and the ferns can then be lifted off. The effect is stunning and very easy to achieve.

## MATERIALS

*wood for the stand (see pattern)*
*tracing paper or transfer paper*
*jig-saw or coping saw*
*wood glue and 2.5 cm / 1 in*
*panel pins*
*hammer*

For the decoration
*shellac*
*household paintbrush*
*newspaper*
*masking tape*
*spray adhesive*
*selection of artificial ferns*
*spray-paint in black, dark green*
*or dark blue*
*fine-grade sandpaper*
*clear matt varnish*

**1**

Apply two coats of shellac to seal and colour the bare wood.

### TO MAKE THE STAND

Cut the timber to the dimensions shown on the pattern in the template section. Mitre the edges. Trace the pattern for the back detail and cut it out using a jig-saw or coping saw. Apply wood glue to all joining edges, join them and then use panel pins to secure them.

**2**

Working on one side at a time, mask off the surrounding area with newspaper and masking tape. Apply mounting spray to one side of the ferns and arrange them on the surface.

**3**

Spray on the colour, using light, even sprays, and building up the colour gradually. Lift the ferns when the paint is dry.

#### 4

Work on all the sides and the inside back panel in the same way.

#### 5

Sand the edges to simulate a time-worn look.

#### 6

Finally, apply two coats of varnish to protect the fernwork.

# Rabbit Dummy Board

*A free-standing oversized rabbit will certainly provide both a focal and a talking point! Dummy boards originated as shop or inn signs; in the days when few people could read, a painted sign would indicate the trade being practised on the premises. The signs would either hang above the doorway or stand on a wooden block. You can give this rabbit a support to make it stand up, or hang it on the wall.*

This project employs a mixture of old and new, as it is an original nineteenth-century engraving enlarged on a photocopier. The fine lines of the original thicken up with enlargement, but not enough to lose the effect of an engraving.

This project is great fun and fairly simple, and the only real skill required is that of cutting the shape out with a jig-saw. Personal experience has shown us that there are people who delight in this; so if you don't have a jig-saw — find someone who does!

## MATERIALS

*wallpaper paste and brush
A2 (59.5 × 42 cm /
23¾ × 16¾ in) sheet of marine
plywood (or similar)
jig-saw
fine-grade sandpaper
shellac
household paintbrushes
varnish in shade 'Antique Pine'
clear matt varnish
scrap of wood for stand
PVA glue*

### 1

Photocopy the rabbit pattern from the template section, enlarging it to the edges of an A4 sheet. Cut the enlargement in half to give two A5 sheets.

### 2

Enlarge both of these up to A3 size. Depending on the machine, this process can be done in one step, or might take several enlargements.

### 3

Apply a coat of wallpaper paste to the plywood. This seals the surface and provides a key for the pasted paper.

### 4

Trim the 'joining' edges of the photocopies right up to the print, so that they can butt up against each other with no overlap. Apply a thin layer of wallpaper paste right up to the edges and stick the two halves together on the board. Smooth out any bubbles with a soft cloth and leave it to dry overnight.

### 5

Use a jig-saw to cut out the shape, leaving a flat base. Using a jig-saw is not difficult, but you will need to practise to get the feel of it. Take your time.

### 6

Sand the edges of the rabbit smooth.

### 7

Seal the surface with a coat of shellac, which will give it a yellowish glow. Apply a coat of Antique Pine varnish, followed by several coats of clear varnish.

### 8

Trace the pattern from the template section. Use it to cut out the stand. Rub down the edges with fine sandpaper and glue in place

# Painted Tin or Tôleware

*Tin-painting reached its zenith in the early days of American settlement, when itinerant merchants would appear in a blaze of colour at farm gates, selling their decorated tin housewares. Even then, they were hard to resist and most homes boasted a display of painted tinware. The word 'tôleware' derives from the French* tôle peinté *meaning 'painted tin', but the style of painting owes more to the Norwegian* rosemaling *than the elaborate French style.*

Our project does not require you to learn the specialized brushstrokes used in traditional tin-painting, although the colours and antiquing will ensure that it blends in well with any other tôleware pieces. These numbered tins were used by tea merchants as containers for different tea blends.

## MATERIALS

*metal primer*
*household paintbrushes*
*large metal tin (either tin or*
*aluminium) with a lid*
*emulsion paint in black,*
*brick-red and maize-yellow*
*selection of artist's brushes*
*tracing paper (optional)*
*soft pencil*
*masking tape*
*hard pencil*
*shellac*
*clear varnish tinted with*
*raw umber acrylic paint*
*clear satin varnish*

### 1

Prime the tin. Paint the lid with black
emulsion and the tin brick-red, with bands
of maize-yellow.

### 2

Trace or photocopy the pattern from the
template section and then cross-hatch over
the back with a soft pencil.

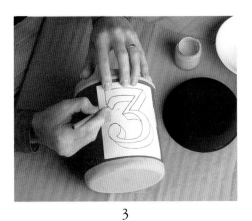

### 3

Use low-tack masking tape to hold the
pattern in position and then draw over it
with a hard pencil, transferring an outline
to the tin.

### 4

Fill in the main body of the '3'
in maize-yellow.

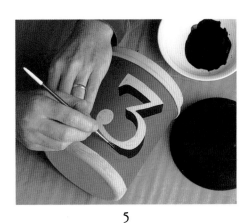

### 5

Fill in the shadow in black.

### 6

Varnish the tin with shellac to give it
a warm glow.

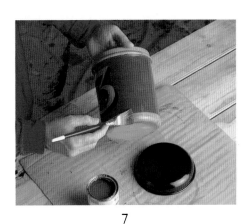

### 7

Apply a coat of tinted varnish and then
give it a coat of clear satin varnish
to protect the surface.

# Curtain-pole Hanging Display

*The Victorian clothes airer made use of the warmth above the range in the days before tumble driers. These days they are seldom used for their original purpose; instead they are adorned with hooks that hold copper pans, baskets and other delights.*

However, not all ceilings are suitable for a heavy airer, and some are not high enough for a hanging display of this sort. For the country look without the creaking timbers and bumped heads, try this attractive, painted curtain pole.

The wooden curtain poles used here can be bought from any DIY store.

MATERIALS

*curtain pole, plus turned finials (not brackets)*
*2 large 'eye' bolts for ceiling beam*
*medium-grade sandpaper*
*emulsion paint in green, red and cream*
*household paintbrushes*
*clear varnish tinted with raw umber acrylic paint*
*2 equal lengths of chain*
*cup hooks and butcher's hooks for displays*

### 1

Using the pole as a measuring guide, position and screw into the ceiling or beam the two 'eye' bolts. These must be very sturdy and firmly fixed. Sand down the pole and finials, and then paint the finials green.

### 2

Paint the pole red. When the pole is dry, paint the cream stripes 6 cm / 2½ in from the ends.

### 3

Sand the paint in places to give an aged look. Fit the finials on the ends of the pole. Apply a coat of tinted varnish. Attach the lengths of chain to the 'eye' bolts. Screw in two cup hooks to the pole in the correct position to line up with the bolts. Attach the butcher's hooks for hanging your decorations, hang up the pole and add your display.

# Embroidered Pelmet

*In France, pelmets such as this one are often pinned up above windows
that do not need curtains, but that would otherwise be too plain.*

The embroidery is simply made from a few basic stitches and is quite suitable for a beginner to attempt. Gingham curtains provide a simple contrast without detracting from the embroidered pattern, but you could make calico curtains and embroider them with the same designs – if you have time and have fallen under the embroidery spell!

## MATERIALS

*tracing paper
dressmaker's transfer paper or
carbon pencil
1 m / 1 yd calico, cut into
2 strips 20 cm / 8 in deep
needle and embroidery thread
in 4 colours
scissors
curtain wire*

1

Enlarge the patterns from the template section to approximately 10 cm / 4 in. Use transfer paper or carbon pencil to transfer the patterns on to the calico.

2

Depending on your knowledge and level of skill, embroider each of the designs. A simple chain-stitch can be used, but cross-stitch, stem-stitch, back-stitch and French knots will add variety.

3

Use satin-stitch to make the scalloped edge. Carefully trim the edge. Sew a seam along the top edge and thread a length of curtain wire through it. Gather to fit the window.

# Trompe-l'oeil Dhurrie

# Canvas Floor Cloth

# Stencilled Border

## Foam-block Painting

## Acorn and
## Oak-leaf Border

11″
28cm

110°

5⅛″
13cm

7½″
19cm

30″
76·25cm

1¾″
4·5cm

## French Bread Bin

# Painted Chest

# Rabbit Dummy Board

# Shelf Bracket and Dummy Board Stand

## Painted Tin Ware

# Embroidered Pelmet

# COUNTRY
# Crafts and
# Flowers

## TESSA EVELEGH

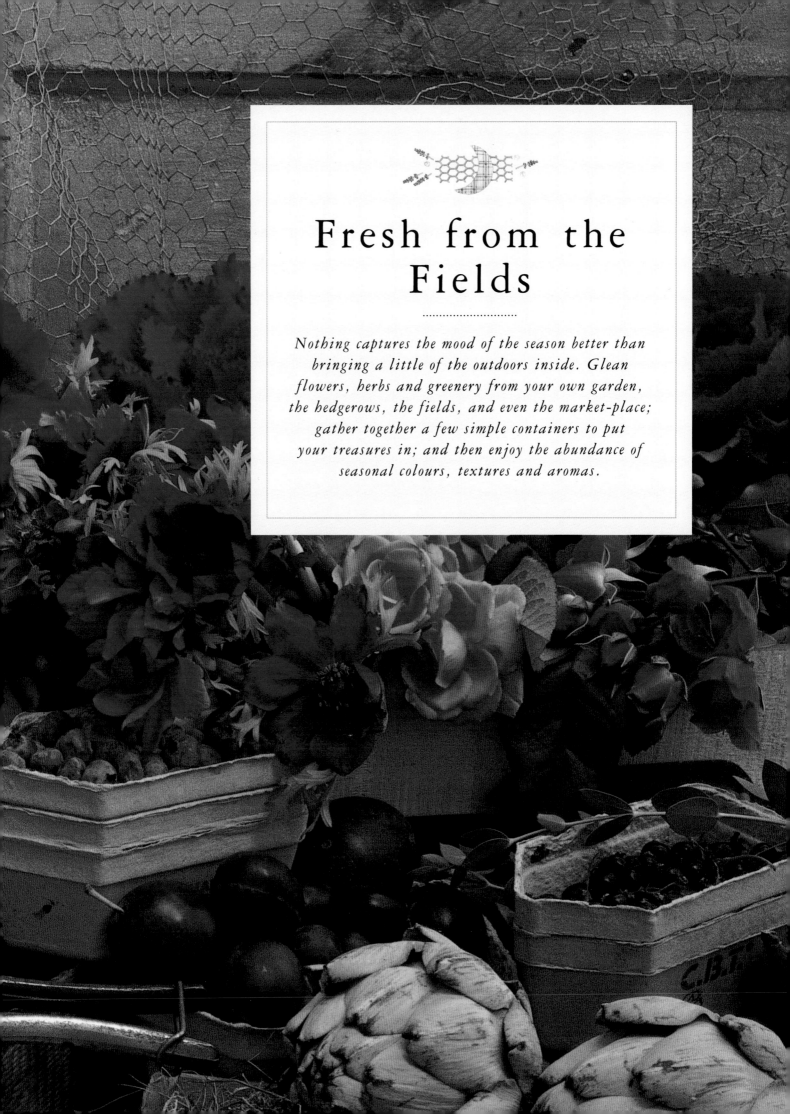

# Fresh from the Fields

........................

*Nothing captures the mood of the season better than
bringing a little of the outdoors inside. Glean
flowers, herbs and greenery from your own garden,
the hedgerows, the fields, and even the market-place;
gather together a few simple containers to put
your treasures in; and then enjoy the abundance of
seasonal colours, textures and aromas.*

# Fresh Herb Wreath

*Gather together a basketful of sweet fresh herbs and make them into an aromatic wreath, to hang in the kitchen or to use as a decorative garland for a celebration. If you choose the fleshier herbs – which hold their moisture – and spray the wreath well, it should last for a couple of days; after this you may wish to dismantle it and dry the individual bunches of herbs.*

## MATERIALS

*florist's wire*
*scissors*
*fresh sage*
*fresh or dried lavender*
*fresh parsley*
*hot glue gun and glue sticks*
*wreath base, about 30 cm / 12 in diameter*
*fresh chives*
*raffia*

### 1

Using the florist's wire, wire all the herbs except the chives into generous bunches.

### 2

Using the glue gun, fix two bunches of sage to the wreath base, stems pointing inwards.

### 3

Next, fix enough lavender bunches side by side to cover the width of the wreath base, hiding the sage stems. Attach bunches of parsley to cover the lavender stems in the same way.

### 4

Work around the wreath base in this way until it is generously covered by the herbs.

### 5

Wire the chives into four generous bunches and trim the cut ends straight. Form each pair into a cross and bind it with raffia. Wire the crosses into position.

### 6

Tie raffia around the wreath at intervals. Make a raffia hanging-loop, thread this on to a generous bundle of raffia at the centre top, and tie the ends of the bundle into a bow to finish.

FRESH FROM THE FIELDS

# Provençal Herb Hanging

*Fix bunches of fresh herbs to a thick plaited rope, add tiny terracotta pots to give
the design structure and then fill it in with garlic and colourful chillies to
make a spicy, herbal gift full of Provençal flavour, for anyone who loves to cook.*

*hank of seagrass string
scissors
garden string
florist's wire
fresh sage
fresh thyme
fresh oregano
2 small flowerpots
6 florist's stub wires
2 garlic heads
hot glue gun and glue sticks (optional)
large dried red chillies*

## 1

Cut six lengths of seagrass string about three
times as long as the desired finished length of
the hanging. Take two lengths, fold them in
half and place them under a length of garden
string. Pass the cut ends over the string and
through the loop of the fold, thereby
knotting the seagrass on to the garden string.
Repeat twice with the remaining four
seagrass lengths. Divide the seagrass into
three bundles of four lengths and plait them
to form the base of the herb hanging.

## 2

Finish the end of the plait by binding it with
a separate piece of seagrass string.

## 3

Using florist's wire, bind the herbs into small
bundles and tie each one with garden string.
Use this to tie them to the plaited base.

## 4

Wire the flowerpots by passing two stub
wires through the central hole and twisting
the ends together.

## 5

Wire the pots to the base by passing a stub
wire through the wires on the pots, passing
it through the plait, and then twisting the
ends together.

## 6

Tie garden string around the garlic heads
and tie these to the base. Wire or glue
the chillies into position, and fill the pots
with more chillies.

# Fresh-flower Fruit Bowl

*Make the prettiest summer fruit bowl by arranging trailing flowers and foliage through a wire basket, topping it with chicken-wire and a pretty plate, and then piling on the fresh fruit. This is a delightful touch for outdoor entertaining.*

## MATERIALS

*jam jar
wire basket
fuchsia flowers or
similar trailing blooms
secateurs
chicken-wire to fit the diameter
of the basket
attractive plate to fit the
diameter of the basket
selection of colourful fruit*

1

Fill the jam jar with water and place it in the centre of the basket.

2

Trim the flower stems with secateurs and arrange them all round the basket by threading the stems through the wire and into the jar of water. Continue until the flowers and foliage provide a delicate curtain of colour around the basket.

3

Cut the chicken-wire to fit over the basket and fix it by bending it around the rim. Place a plate on this chicken-wire, and then fill the plate with colourful summer fruits.

# Vegetable Centrepiece

*The flower stall is not the only source of material for centrepieces — the vegetable stall provides great pickings, too. Here, a still-life of ornamental cabbages — complemented by a simple cut-open red cabbage and some artichokes — makes a flamboyant focal-point for the table. The theme is carried through by adding an ornamental cabbage leaf to the cutlery bundle at each setting.*

## MATERIALS

*dyed raffia*
*painted wooden basket*
*2 ornamental cabbages in pots*
*lichen moss*
*1 set of cutlery and napkin*
*per person*
*baby-food jar*
*painted trug*
*red cabbage, halved*
*globe artichokes*

### 1

Tie a bow of dyed raffia around the handle of the wooden basket. Remove several perfect cabbage leaves and place the cabbages in their pots in the basket.

### 2

Cover the tops of the pots with silvery-grey lichen moss.

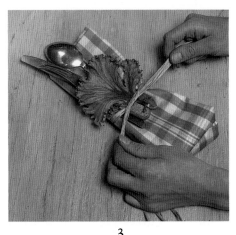

### 3

Tie up each cutlery bundle with a napkin and an ornamental cabbage leaf. Finish the arrangement by putting a few more leaves into a baby-food jar and tying dyed raffia around it. Fill a garden trug with the red cabbage halves and the globe artichokes.

# Candle Centrepiece

*Even the humblest materials can be put together to make an elegant centrepiece.
The garden shed has been raided for this one, which is made from a terracotta
flowerpot and chicken-wire. Fill it up with red berries, ivies and white roses
for a rich, Christmassy look; or substitute seasonal flowers and foliage
at any other time of the year.*

### MATERIALS

*18 cm / 7 in flowerpot
about 1 m / 39 in chicken-wire
knife
florist's foam ball to fit
the diameter of the pot*

*beeswax candle
tree ivy
white roses
berries
variegated trailing ivy*

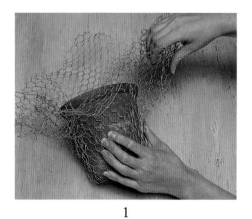

**1**

Place the pot in the centre of a large square
of chicken-wire. Bring the chicken-wire up
around the pot and bend it into position.

**2**

Cut the florist's foam ball in half and soak
one half. The other half isn't needed.

**3**

Place the foam in the pot, cut-side up
so you have a flat surface. Position the candle
in the centre of the pot.

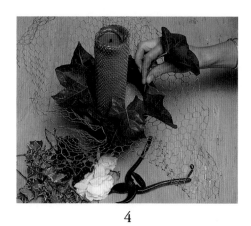

**4**

Arrange glossy tree-ivy leaves all around the
candle, to provide a lush green base.

**5**

Add a white rose as a focal point, and
bunches of red berries among the ivy.

**6**

Add more white roses, and intersperse
trailing variegated ivy among the tree ivy.

# Wild at Heart

*Often, the simplest arrangements are the most appealing. Here, flowers are arranged very simply in little glass jars wound around with blue twine and carefully grouped to make a delightful still-life.*

## MATERIALS

| | |
|---|---|
| *blue twine* | *scabious* |
| *2 jam jars* | *anemones* |
| *secateurs* | *glass plate* |

### 1

Wrap the blue twine around the jars and tie securely. Fill the jars with water.

### 2

Fill one jar with scabious and another with anemones, cutting the stems to the right lengths as you go.

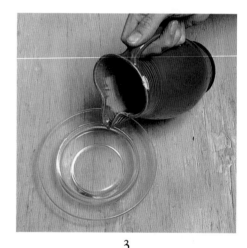

### 3

Fill the plate with water.

### 4

Cut one of the flower stems very short and allow the bloom to float in the plate. This is a delightful solution for any heads of flowers that have broken off during transit.

# Advent Candle Ring

*An Advent candle ring makes a pretty Christmas centrepiece. This one — decorated with glossy green tree ivy, Cape gooseberries, dried citrus-fruit slices and bundles of cinnamon sticks — is a delight to the eye, while giving off a rich seasonal aroma.*

## MATERIALS

*florist's foam*
*knife*
*florist's ring basket*
*4 church candles*
*moss*
*dried orange slices*
*florist's stub wires*
*secateurs*
*cinnamon sticks*
*golden twine*
*tree ivy*
*Cape gooseberries*

**1**

Soak the florist's foam and cut it to fit the ring basket.

**2**

Position the candles in the foam.

**3**

Cover the florist's foam with moss, pushing it well down at the sides of the basket.

**4**

Wire the orange slices by passing a stub wire through the centre, and then twisting the ends together at the outside edge. Wire the cinnamon sticks into bundles, then tie them with golden twine and then pass a wire through the string.

**5**

Wire the tree-ivy leaves into bundles.

**6**

Position the ivy leaves into the ring. Decorate by fixing in the orange slices and cinnamon sticks and placing the Cape gooseberries on top of the candle ring at intervals.

# Autumn Fruitfulness

*The sheer beauty of autumn produce makes it difficult to resist. It's too good to be left in the larder. Gather together all the softly bloomed purple fruits and pile them into a rich seasonal display for a side table or centrepiece.*

## MATERIALS

*metal urn
filling material, such as
bubble-wrap, newspaper or
florist's foam
several varieties of plums
black grapes
hydrangea heads
globe artichokes
blueberries*

### 1

Unless you have a huge abundance of fruit,
fill the bottom of the urn with bubble-wrap,
newspaper or florist's foam.

### 2

Arrange as many different varieties of plums
as you can find on the filling, saving a few
for the final decoration.

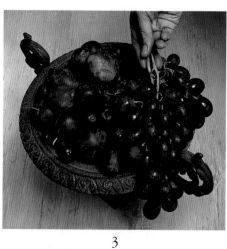

### 3

Add a large bunch of black grapes, draping
them over the rim of the urn. Finish the
arrangement with hydrangea heads,
artichokes, scattered plums and blueberries.

# Autumn Gold

*The golds of autumn can be gathered into a fabulous display, using even the humblest of containers. Here, the dahlias have simply been put into a store-cupboard Kilner jar and given a seasonal necklace of hazelnuts.*

## MATERIALS

*hazelnuts*
*seagrass string*
*secateurs*
*dahlias*
*Kilner jar*
*pumpkins*
*branches of pyracantha*
*with berries*

### 1

Tie the hazelnuts on to the seagrass string
to make a 'necklace'.

### 2

Cut about 1 cm / ½ in off the end of each
dahlia stem and place the stems in the
Kilner jar filled with water.

### 3

Tie the hazelnut 'necklace' around the jar.
Finish the arrangement with pumpkins
and pyracantha branches.

# Springtime Garland

*Garlands of fresh flowers make delightful decorations for any celebration.*
*This pretty little hanging of pansies and violas has a woodland feel that can be*
*re-created at any time, because these flowers are available in*
*most months of the year.*

## MATERIALS

*secateurs*
*chicken-wire the desired length of*
*the garland and three times the*
*desired width*
*scissors*
*black plastic bin liner*
*about two pansy plants for every*
*15 cm / 6 in of garland*
*about six viola plants for every*
*15 cm / 6 in of garland*
*florist's stub wires*
*moss*

1

Using secateurs, cut the chicken-wire to size
and then form it into a flattened roll.

2

Cut the bin liner into squares large enough
to cover the rootballs of the pansies
and violas.

3

One by one, unpot each plant, gently remove
any loose soil and place the rootball in
the centre of a square of bin liner.

### 4

Gather the plastic around the rootball and
fix it in place by winding stub wires loosely
round the top, leaving a short length free
to fix to the garland.

### 5

Fix the bagged-up plants to the garland
using the free end of wire.

### 6

Finish off by covering any visible plastic with
moss, fixing it with short lengths of florist's
stub wire bent hairpin-style.

# Summer Gift Basket

*Fresh flowers are always a welcome gift — make them into something extra special by laying them in a basket with prettily packaged, home-made strawberry jam.*

MATERIALS

*jar of strawberry jam*
*pink paper*
*glue*
*paper strawberry print*
*scissors*
*glazed pink paper*
*raffia*
*wooden basket*
*coloured paper*
*roses*

### 1

Make up a pretty presentation for the strawberry jam by wrapping the jar with pink paper and gluing on a paper strawberry print to fix the paper.

### 2

Make a top of glazed pink paper and a raffia tie. Line the basket with coloured paper and fill it with a bunch of roses, tied with raffia, and the strawberry jam.

# Christmas Gift Basket

*Decorate a willow basket with gilded ivy leaves, and then pack it with seasonal goodies: a pot of variegated ivies and berries, decorative florist's pineapples, plus a few extra treats like beeswax candles and crystallized fruits.*

MATERIALS

*tree ivy*
*picture framer's wax gilt*
*willow basket*
*scissors*
*hessian*
*pot of variegated ivy with berries*
*presents*

1

Gild the tree ivy by rubbing on picture framer's wax gilt, using your fingers. Decorate the rim of the basket with these gilded leaves.

2

Cut a piece of hessian to size and fray the edges. Use it to line the basket. Add the pot of ivy, plus presents to fill the basket.

# Twiggy Door Wreath

*Welcome seasonal guests with a door wreath that's charming in its simplicity.*
*Just bend twigs into a heart shape and adorn the heart with variegated ivy,*
*berries and a Christmas rose, or substitute any pure-white rose.*

## MATERIALS

*secateurs*
*pliable branches, such as*
*buddleia, cut from the garden*
*florist's wire*
*seagrass string*
*variegated trailing ivy*
*red berries*
*tree ivy*
*picture framer's wax gilt*
*(optional)*
*white rose*
*golden twine*

### 1

Using secateurs, cut six lengths of pliable
branches about 70 cm / 28 in long.
Wire three together at one end. Repeat with
the other three. Cross the two bundles over
at the wired end.

### 2

Wire the bunches together in the
crossed-over position.

### 3

Holding the crossed, wired ends with one
hand, ease the long end round and down
very gently, so the branches don't snap.
Repeat with the other side, to form a heart
shape. Wire the bottom end of the heart.

### 4

Bind the wiring with seagrass string at top
and bottom and make a hanging loop
at the top.

### 5

Entwine trailing ivy around the heart shape.

### 6

Add berries. Make a posy of tree-ivy leaves
(if you like, gild them using picture framer's
wax gilt) and a white rose. Tie the posy with
golden twine. Wire the posy in position at
the top of the heart.

**FRESH FROM THE FIELDS**

..........................

# Tied Posy

*Flowers are at their most appealing when kept simple. Just gather together some garden cuttings and arrange them in a pretty posy that the recipient can simply unwrap and put straight into a vase, without further ado.*

MATERIALS

| | |
|---|---|
| secateurs | scabious |
| roses | brown paper |
| eucalyptus | ribbon |

**1**

Using secateurs, cut each flower stem to approximately 15 cm / 6 in long.

**2**

Gather the flowers together, surrounding each rose with some feathery eucalyptus, and then adding the scabious.

**3**

Wrap the posy with paper and tie it with a pretty ribbon bow.

# Tussie Mussie

*Traditionally, tussie mussies were bouquets of concentrically arranged aromatic herbs that were carried around as a personal perfume. This one combines the blue-greens of sage and thyme with the soft blues of lavender and scabious flowers.*

MATERIALS

*6 scabious*
*fresh thyme*
*fresh lavender*
*fresh sage*
*dyed raffia*

**1**

Encircle the scabious blooms
with fresh thyme.

**2**

Arrange a circle of lavender around this,
making sure the piece keeps its circular shape.

**3**

Add a circle of sage, then tie with a
generous bundle of dyed raffia.

# Easter Display

*Coloured eggs immediately transform springtime flowers into an Easter display.
Simplicity is the secret: just gather together an abundance of flowers and add a
few eggs, carefully laid on to moss to evoke the idea of a nest.*

## MATERIALS

*hard-boiled eggs
food dye if you want to eat the
eggs, or fabric dye if they are
purely for decoration
one jam jar for each colour
vinegar
salt
secateurs
tulips or any spring flowers
vase
moss
plate*

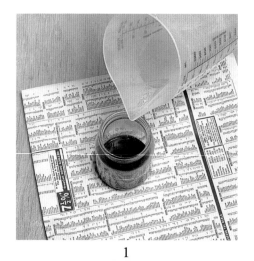

### 1

First wash the eggs, and then make up the
dye. Do this by emptying half a small bottle
of food dye or half a disc of fabric dye into a
jam jar, and then pouring on 300 ml /
½ pint / 1¼ cups of hot water.

### 2

Add 30 ml / 2 tbsp vinegar and 15 ml / 1 tbsp
salt. Lower an egg into the jam jar of dye
and leave it for a few minutes.
Check the colour regularly.

### 3

When the egg has reached the desired colour,
lift it out and repeat with the rest. You will
find that the more eggs you dye, the weaker
the solution will become, so you'll have to
leave the eggs in longer to achieve the
same effect. Cut about 1 cm / ½ in off the end
of each flower stem with secateurs, and
then place them in a vase. Complete the
arrangement by arranging the eggs on the
moss on a plate.

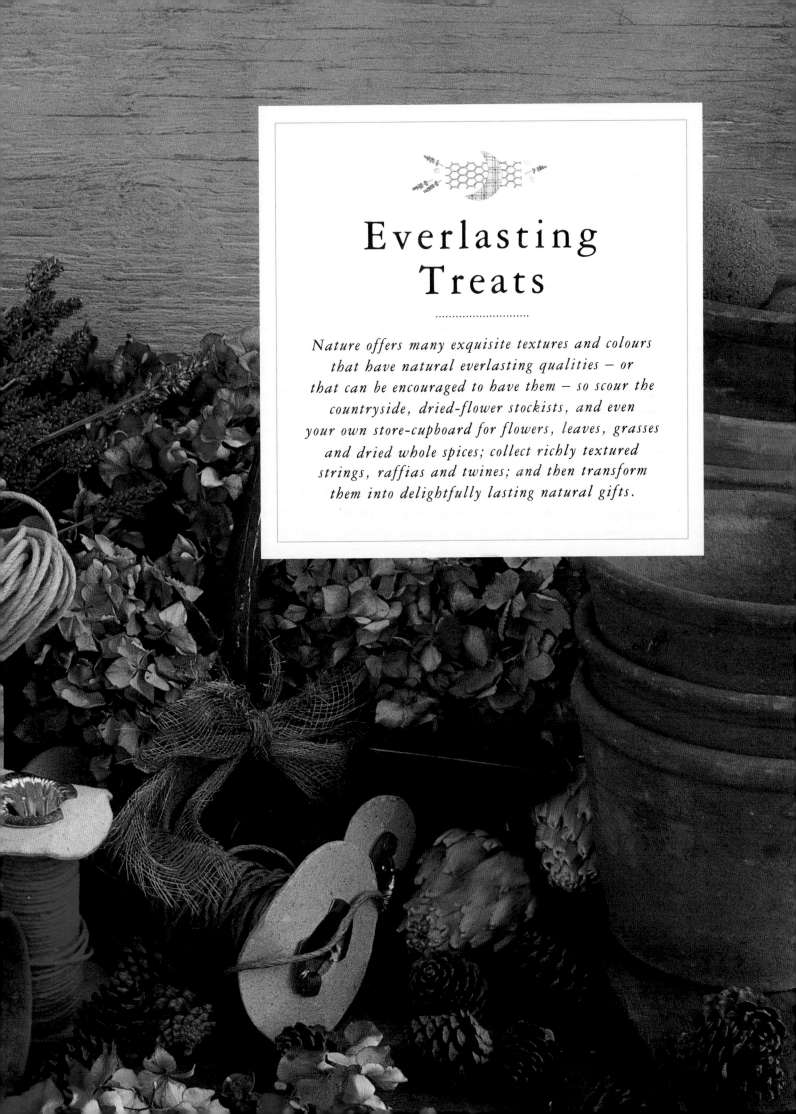

# Everlasting Treats

Nature offers many exquisite textures and colours
that have natural everlasting qualities — or
that can be encouraged to have them — so scour the
countryside, dried-flower stockists, and even
your own store-cupboard for flowers, leaves, grasses
and dried whole spices; collect richly textured
strings, raffias and twines; and then transform
them into delightfully lasting natural gifts.

# Lavender Basket

*A basket decorated with bunches of dried lavender makes an exquisitely pretty aromatic linen store. It could also be kept on the kitchen dresser, filled with freshly laundered tea towels ready on hand when you need them.*

## MATERIALS

*dried lavender (2 bunches for the handle plus about 1 bunch for every 10 cm / 4 in of basket rim)*

*florist's wire
scissors
willow basket*

*hot glue gun and glue sticks
blue paper-ribbon
blue twine*

#### 1

Wire up enough small bundles of about six lavender heads to cover the rim of the basket generously. Arrange the heads so they are staggered to give fuller cover. Trim the stalks short.

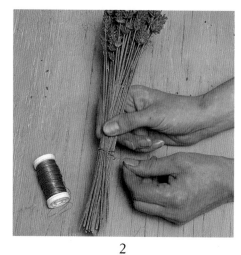

#### 2

Wire up the remaining lavender into 12 larger bunches of about 12 lavender heads for the handles, leaving the stalks long.

#### 3

Form a 'star' of three of the larger bunches and wire them together. Repeat with the other nine so you have four largish star-shaped bunches of lavender.

#### 4

Fix the small bunches to the rim of the basket, using either wire or hot glue in a glue gun. Start at one end and work towards the handle. Use the bunches generously so they overlap each other to cover the width of the rim.

#### 5

Once the rim is fully covered, glue on individual heads of lavender to cover any spaces, ugly wires or stalks. Pay particular attention to the area near the handles, because you will have finished up with quite a few bare stalks there.

#### 6

Wind blue paper-ribbon around the handle. Wire the longer lavender bunches to the handles, leaving the stalks long but trimming to neaten them. Cut the stalks on the inside of the handle shorter to fit the space. Bind the wired joints with blue twine.

# Heart of Wheat

*Fashion a heart at harvest time, when wheat is plentiful, for a delightful decoration that would look good adorning a wall or a dresser at any time of the year. Despite its delicate feathery looks, this heart is quite robust and should last many years.*

## MATERIALS

*scissors*
*heavy-gauge garden wire*
*or similar*
*florist's tape*
*florist's wire*
*large bundle of wheat ears*

### 1

Cut three long lengths of heavy-gauge wire and bend them into a heart shape. Twist the ends together at the bottom.

### 2

Use florist's tape to bind the wire heart shape.

### 3

Using florist's wire, make up enough small bundles of wheat ears to cover the wire heart shape densely. Leave a short length of wire at each end for fixing to the heart shape.

### 4

Starting at the bottom, tape the first bundle of wheat ears to the heart.

### 5

Place the second bundle further up the heart shape behind the first, and tape it in position. Continue until the whole heart is covered.

### 6

For the bottom, wire together about six bunches of wheat ears, twist the wires together and wire them to the heart, finishing off with florist's tape to neaten. This is what the back should look like by the time you've finished.

# Flower Topiary

*Dried flowers look fabulous when given the sculptural form of* faux *topiary.*
*These strawflowers and larkspur set into a tall cone make a stunning everlasting*
*display. Wrap the pot in a co-ordinating fabric to finish off the arrangement.*

## MATERIALS

*small flowerpot*
*square of fabric to cover the pot*
*knife*
*small florist's dry foam cone*
*4 florist's stub wires*
*florist's dry foam cone,*
*about 18 cm / 7 in tall*
*scissors*
*bunch of dried blue larkspur*
*florist's wire, if necessary*
*bunch of dried*
*yellow strawflowers*

1

Stand the pot in the centre of the fabric and
tuck the corners into the pot. Tuck in any
other loose portions of fabric.

2

Cut down the small foam cone to fit the
inside of the pot. Position four stub wires
so they project above the foam. Use these
for attaching the top cone.

3

Snip the florets off the larkspur, leaving the
small stalks to push into the foam. Make four
rows of larkspur down the length of the cone
to quarter it; then fill in either side of these
rows to create broad blue bands. Many of the
florets' stalks will be strong enough to pierce
the foam. If not, wire the florets with
florist's wire. Finally, fill in the panels
with the strawflowers.

# Leaf and Petal Decorations

*Decorations are so much more appealing when made from all things natural.*
*These, made from preserved oak and beech leaves and dried hydrangea flowers,*
*are easy to do, and they make delightful tree or table decorations.*

## MATERIALS

*scissors*
*dried mop-head hydrangeas*
*(about two for every ball)*
*hot glue gun and glue sticks*
*florist's dry foam balls, about*
*7.5 cm / 3 in in diameter*
*glycerined beech leaves*
*glycerined or dyed, dried*
*oak leaves*
*picture framer's wax gilt*

**1**

Snip the florets off the mop-head hydrangeas.
Put aside the florets that have the prettiest
colouring on the top-side of the petals. Leave
a little stalk on these, but trim the stalks off
the rest. Carefully glue a floret top-side
down on to a florist's ball.

**2**

Continue to glue the florets face downwards
until the ball is completely covered.

**3**

Put a tiny spot of glue on the back of each of
the petals of a reserved floret. Fix this,
top-side up, on to the ball – over the base
covering of petals. If you leave a little stalk
on the florets you set aside for the top layer,
this can be used to help attach it to the ball.
Let the glue work just where the petals touch
the ball, allowing them to curl naturally at
the edges to provide texture. Continue until
the ball is covered. To make the leaf balls,
first gild the beech leaves with wax gilt.
Stick the beech and oak leaves over the ball,
overlapping them slightly to cover the foam.

# Hydrangea Pot

*Dried materials can be used to make the simplest, yet most exquisite, gifts. Here's an easy but effective idea, using a single hydrangea head.*

### MATERIALS

*glue
dyed, dried oak leaf
small flowerpot
dyed raffia
scissors
dried mop-head hydrangea*

1

Use a spot of glue to attach the leaf to the pot, and then tie it on with raffia. Secure the raffia tie at the back with another spot of glue.

2

Cut the hydrangea stalk short enough so that the head rests on the pot. Place the head in the pot.

# Spice Pots

*For a cook, make a cornucopia of culinary flavourings by putting different dried herbs and spices into terracotta pots and packing the pots in a wire basket.*

### MATERIALS

*cinnamon sticks
dried bay leaves
garlic
dried red chillies
small flowerpots
wire basket
wire
raffia*

1

Place the herbs and spices in the pots and place the pots in the basket.

2

Bend a piece of wire into a heart shape and bind it with raffia. Leave a long end free before starting to bind. When binding is complete, the end can be used to tie the heart to the basket. Finish with a bow.

# Leafy Pictures

*Delicate skeletonized leaves come in such breathtakingly exquisite forms that
they deserve to be shown off. Mount them on hand-made papers and frame them
to make simple yet stunning natural collages.*

## MATERIALS

*wooden picture frame
sandpaper
paint
paintbrush
backing paper
pencil
scissors
skeletonized leaf
picture framer's wax gilt
hot glue gun and glue sticks
mounting paper*

### 1

Take the frame apart and sand it down to
provide a key before painting. A translucent
colourwash has been used for painting here,
but any paint will do.

### 2

Allow the paint to dry, then sand the
paint back so you're left with a wooden frame
with shading in the mouldings, plus a
veil of colour on the surface.

### 3

Use the hardboard back of the frame as a
template for the backing paper. Draw around
it with a pencil to form a cutting line.

### 4

Cut the backing paper out.

5

Prepare the leaf by rubbing with picture framer's wax gilt. This does take a little time as the gilt has to be well worked in.

6

Stick the backing paper on the frame back, glue the mounting paper in the centre and attach the leaf on to that. Here, the leaf is centred with the stalk breaking the edge of the mounting paper. Finally, put the frame back together.

# Natural Christmas Decorations

*Raid the store-cupboard and scrap box, add garden clippings plus dried fruit slices, and you have the ingredients for delightful Christmas decorations that can be individually hung or tied on to the tree, or strung on to twine to make a garland.*

## MATERIALS

*florist's stub wires*
*bundles of twigs*
*picture framer's wax gilt*
*dried bay leaves*
*dried pear slices*
*fabric scraps*
*dried apple slices*
*dried orange slices*
*small elastic bands*
*cinnamon sticks*
*gold twine*
*beeswax candle ends*

### 1

Wire together bundles of twigs, and then gild them by rubbing in picture framer's wax gilt.

### 2

Make up the fruit bundles. Make a small loop at one end of a florist's stub wire. Thread on some dried bay leaves, and then a dried pear, passing the wire through the rind at the top and bottom. Make a hook at the top.

### 3

Tie a scrap of coloured fabric to the bottom loop and a scrap of green (synthetic chiffon is shown) at the top, to look like leaves. Make the apple-slice bundles by threading on first the thick apple slices, and then the bay leaves.

### 4

Wire up pairs of thinner-sliced apples by passing a wire through the centre and twisting the wires together at the top. Wire up the orange slices in the same way.

### 5

Use small elastic bands to make up bundles of cinnamon sticks.

### 6

Either hang each decoration directly on the tree or make up a garland to hang on the tree or at the window. Here, they have been strung together using gold twine. The beeswax candle-ends are simply knotted in at intervals.

# Everlasting Christmas Tree

*This delightful little tree, made from dyed, preserved oak leaves and decorated with tiny gilded cones, would make an enchanting Christmas decoration. Make several and then group them to make a centrepiece, or place one at each setting.*

*knife*
*bunch of dyed, dried oak leaves*
*florist's wire*
*small fir cones*
*picture framer's wax gilt*
*flowerpot, 18 cm / 7 in tall*
*small florist's dry foam cone*
*4 florist's stub wires*
*florist's dry foam cone,*
*about 18 cm / 7 in tall*

### 1

Cut the leaves off the branches and trim the stalks. Wire up bunches of about four leaves, making some bunches with small leaves, some with medium-sized leaves and others with large leaves. Sort the bunches into piles.

### 3

Prepare the pot by cutting the smaller foam cone to fit the pot, adding stub-wire stakes and positioning the larger cone on to this. Attach the leaves to the cone, starting at the top with the bunches of small leaves, and working down through the medium and large leaves to make a realistic shape. Add the gilded cones to finish.

### 2

Insert wires into the bottom end of each fir cone and twist the ends together. Gild each cone by rubbing on wax gilt.

# Fruity Tree

*Glycerined leaves make a perfect foundation for any dried topiary. You can buy
them in branches, ready glycerined for use, or glycerine your own garden
prunings. Here, they have been wired into bunches for a fabulous, full look.*

### MATERIALS

*secateurs
3 branches of glycerined
beech leaves
florist's stub wires
dried pear slices
florist's dry foam ball, about
13 cm / 5 in diameter
flowerpot, 18 cm / 7 in tall*

#### 1

Cut the leaves off the branches and trim the
stalks short. Wire up small bunches of
four or six beech leaves and twist the ends
of the wires together.

#### 2

Pass a stub wire through the top of each pear
slice and twist the ends together.

#### 3

Completely cover the portion of the ball that
will show above the pot with beech leaves.

#### 4

Add the pear slices and put the ball
into the pot.

E V E R L A S T I N G   T R E A T S
.............................

# Spice Topiary

*Fashion a delightfully aromatic, culinary topiary from cloves and star anise, pot it in terracotta decorated with cinnamon sticks and top with a cinnamon-stick cross. Sticking all the cloves into the florist's foam is both easy to do and wonderfully therapeutic.*

## MATERIALS

*small 'long Tom'
flowerpot
knife
cinnamon sticks
hot glue gun and glue sticks
florist's dry foam cone,
about 23 cm / 9 in tall
small florist's dry foam cone
florist's stub wires
large pack of star anise
cloves*

**1**

Prepare the pot by cutting the cinnamon sticks to the length of the pot and gluing them in position.

**2**

Trim the top of the larger cone. Cut the smaller cone to fit inside the pot. Put four stub-wires upright in the pot so they project above the foam.

**3**

Use the stub-wires to stake the trimmed cone on top of the foam-filled pot.

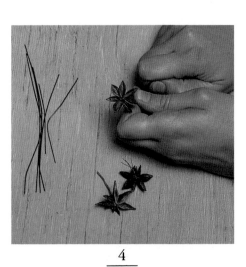

**4**

Sort out all the complete star anise from the pack, plus any that are almost complete — you'll need about 20 in all. Wire these up by passing a wire over the front in one direction, and another wire over the front in another direction to make a cross of wires. Twist the wires together at the back and trim to about 1 cm / ½ in.

##### 5

Start by arranging the star anise in rows
down the cone – about three each side to
quarter the cone. Put two vertically between
each line. Next, just fill the whole remaining
area of cone with cloves, packing them
tightly so none of the foam shows through.

##### 6

Glue two short pieces of cinnamon stick
into a cross. Wire this up, and use it
to decorate the top.

# Dried-flower Pot

*Dried flowers always look their best when the blooms are massed and the stalks not too prominent. Here's a charming treatment: roses and lavender tucked into a tiny terracotta pot, and then tied around with raffia.*

MATERIALS

*knife*
*small florist's dry foam cone*
*small 'long Tom' flowerpot*
*dried rosebuds*
*scissors or secateurs*
*dried lavender*
*dyed raffia*
*hot glue gun and glue sticks*

**1**

Trim the foam to fit the pot. Place the rosebuds around the edge of the pot.

**2**

Cut the lavender stalks to about 1 cm / ½ in and use them to fill the centre of the arrangement. Tie a dyed raffia bow around the pot and secure it at the back with a spot of glue.

# Everlasting Basket

*Hydrangeas look fabulous dried, providing a flamboyant display that can simply be massed into a basket. They're also about the easiest flowers to dry at home. Just put the cut flowers in about 1 cm / ½ in of water and leave them. The flowers will take up the water and then gradually dry out.*

### MATERIALS

*knife*
*florist's dry foam*
*painted wooden basket*
*dried mop-head hydrangeas*
*dried globe artichokes*
*ribbon*

### 1

Cut the florist's foam to fit and fill the basket, and then arrange the hydrangeas to cover the top of the basket.

### 2

Add the dried globe artichoke at one end for texture.

### 3

Tie a ribbon to the handle of the basket to finish.

# Dried-herb Wreath

*A dried-herb wreath based on lavender makes a wonderful, textural, aromatic wall hanging. This one also incorporates mugwort, tarragon, lovage and large French lavender seedheads.*

## MATERIALS

*scissors
florist's wire
dried lavender
dried mugwort
dried lovage
dried tarragon
hot glue gun and glue sticks
small wreath base
French lavender seedheads*

### 1

Wire all the dried herbs and flowers, except the French lavender seedheads, into small bunches.

### 2

Using a glue gun, fix a bunch of lavender to the wreath base.

### 3

Next, glue a bunch of mugwort to the wreath base.

### 4

Work round the base, adding a bunch of lovage.

### 5

Continue all round the wreath, interspersing the different bunches of herbs to cover it completely, using the tarragon to add a feathery look.

### 6

Finally, for structure, add the individual French lavender seedheads.

# Love and Kisses Collage

*This witty natural collage is made from tropical seedheads and cinnamon sticks mounted on linen muslin. Even the frame has been decorated with giant cinnamon sticks, glued over a simple wooden one.*

## MATERIALS

*wooden picture frame*
*brown backing paper*
*scissors*
*linen muslin*
*hot glue gun and glue sticks*
*knife*
*small cinnamon sticks*
*florist's wire*
*heart-shaped or any other large tropical seedheads*
*4 huge cinnamon sticks*

### 1

Take the glass out of the picture frame and stick the backing paper to the hardboard backing. Cut the linen muslin to size, and fray the edges. Put spots of glue all around the edge of the muslin and then stick it to the backing.

### 2

Glue six short lengths of cinnamon into three crosses, and then wire them up to form a delicate metallic cross joint.

### 3

Glue the heart-shaped seedheads to the top of the picture; glue the cinnamon 'kisses' to the bottom.

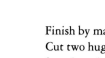

### 4

Finish by making a cinnamon-stick frame. Cut two huge cinnamon sticks to the same length as the frame and two to the same as the width. First glue a stick to the top of the frame, and then one to the bottom. Next, glue the side ones to these.

# Decorative Dried Artichokes

*The exquisite pinky shades at the base of some dried globe artichokes are too beautiful to be covered up by containers. Show them off by balancing the artichokes across pots covered in linen muslin to make wonderful natural decorations.*

## MATERIALS

*small flowerpot*
*square of linen muslin*
*dyed raffia*
*dried globe artichokes with*
*a pinky-purple hue*

### 1

Place the pot in the centre of the linen muslin and tuck the fabric corners into the pot.

### 2

Tuck in any other loose ends, and then tie everything in place with raffia. Make an arrangement by balancing the artichokes on the pot to show off the depth of colour on the undersides.

# Spicy Pomander

*Pomanders were originally nature's own air fresheners. The traditional orange pomanders are fairly tricky to do, because the critical drying process can so easily go wrong, leading to mouldy oranges. This one, made of cloves and cardamom pods offers none of those problems, and makes a refreshing change in soft muted colours.*

MATERIALS

*cloves
florist's dry foam ball,
about 7.5 cm / 3 in diameter
hot glue gun and glue sticks
green cardamom pods
raffia
florist's stub wire*

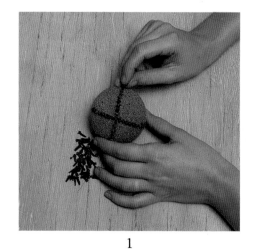

1

Start by making a single line of cloves all around the circumference of the ball. Make another one in the other direction, so you have divided the ball into quarters.

2

Make a line of cloves on both sides of the original lines to make broad bands of cloves quartering the ball.

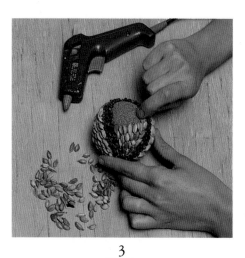

3

Starting at the top of the first quarter, glue cardamom pods over the foam, methodically working in rows to create a neat effect. Repeat on the other three quarters.

4

Tie a bow in the centre of a length of raffia. Pass a stub wire through the knot and twist the ends together.

**5**

Fix the bow to the top of the ball
using the stub wire.

**6**

Join the two loose ends in a knot
for hanging the pomander.

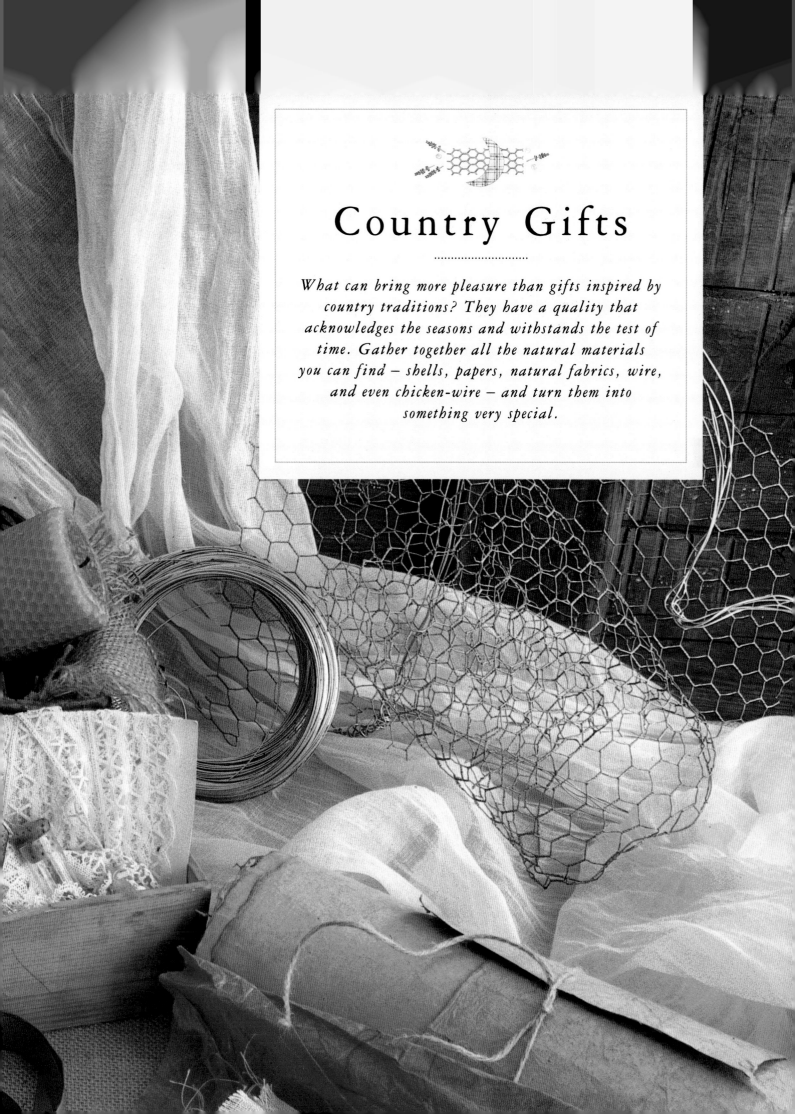

# Country Gifts

....................

*What can bring more pleasure than gifts inspired by country traditions? They have a quality that acknowledges the seasons and withstands the test of time. Gather together all the natural materials you can find — shells, papers, natural fabrics, wire, and even chicken-wire — and turn them into something very special.*

# Sleep Pillow

*Many people still swear by sleep pillows, which are traditionally filled with chamomile and hops. Since hops are related to the cannabis plant, they induce a feeling of sleepy well-being, while chamomile helps you to relax. Either buy ready-prepared sleep mix, or make up your own with chamomile, lemon verbena and a few hops. Stitch a pillow filled with these relaxing herbs to keep on your bed, and look forward to some good night's sleep.*

MATERIALS

*linen muslin, 2 m × 20 cm /
80 × 8 in (this can be made up
of two or more shorter lengths)
pins, needle and thread
scissors
pure cotton fabric, 50 × 25 cm /
20 × 10 in
herbal sleep mix
1 m / 39 in antique lace
1 m / 39 in ribbon,
1 cm / ½ in wide
4 pearl buttons*

<u>1</u>

Prepare the linen muslin border by stitching together enough lengths to make up 2 m / 80 in. With right sides facing, stitch the ends together to form a ring. Trim the seam. Fold the ring in half lengthways with wrong sides facing and run a line of gathering stitches close to the raw edges.

<u>2</u>

Cut two pieces of cotton fabric into 25 cm / 10 in squares. Pull up the gathering threads of the muslin to fit the cushion edge. Pin it to the right side of one square, with raw edges facing outwards, matching the raw edges and easing the gathers evenly round the cushion. Put the second square on top and pin the corners. Stitch the seams, leaving a gap for stuffing. Trim the seams.

<u>3</u>

Turn the cushion right-side out and fill it with herbal sleep mix. Stitch the gap to enclose the border.

**4**

Using tiny stitches, sew the lace to the
cushion about 2.5 cm / 1 in away
from the border.

**5**

Stitch the ribbon close to the lace, making
a neat diagonal fold at the corners.

**6**

Finish by sewing a tiny pearl button
to each corner.

# Herb Pot-mat

*Protect tabletops from hot pots and pans with an aromatic mat, filled with cinnamon, cloves and bay leaves. The heat of the pot immediately releases the piquancy of its contents, kept evenly distributed with mattress-style ties.*

## MATERIALS

scissors
ticking, at least 62 × 55 cm /
25 × 22 in
pins, needle and thread

spice mix to fill, e.g. dried bay
leaves, cloves, cinnamon sticks
heavy-duty upholstery needle
cotton string

### 1

First make the hanger by cutting a strip of ticking 5 × 30 cm / 2 × 12 in. With right sides facing, fold this in half lengthways. Stitch the long side, leaving the ends open. Trim the seam. Turn right side out and press. Fold in half to form a loop. Cut two rectangles from the fabric measuring about 62 × 50 cm / 25 × 20 in.

### 2

Place the cushion pieces on a flat surface, right sides facing, and then slip the hanging loop between the layers, with the raw edges pointing out towards a corner.

### 3

Pin and stitch the cushion pieces together, leaving about 7.5 cm / 3 in open. Trim the seams. Turn right side out.

### 4

Fill the cushion with the spices.

### 5

Slip-stitch to close the opening.

### 6

Using a heavy-duty upholstery needle threaded with cotton string, make a stitch about a third in from two sides of the cushion, clearing the spices inside the mat away from the area as you go. Untwist the strands of the string for a more feathery look. Repeat with three other ties to give a mattress effect. Make a simple knot in each to secure the ties.

# Lavender Sachets

*Use fabric scraps to appliqué simple motifs on to charming chequered fabrics, and then stitch them into sachets to fill with lavender and use as drawer-fresheners. Inspired by traditional folk art, these have universal appeal.*

### MATERIALS
*scissors
fabric scraps
paper for templates
pins, needle and thread
stranded embroidery thread in
different colours
loose dried lavender
button*

### 1

Cut two pieces of fabric into squares about 15 cm / 6 in. If you are using a checked or striped fabric, it is a good idea to let the design dictate the exact size. Scale up the template and use it as a pattern to cut bird and wing shapes from contrasting fabrics. Pin and tack the bird shape to the right side of one square.

### 2

Neatly slip-stitch the bird shape to the sachet front, turning in the edges as you go. Repeat with the wing shape.

### 3

Using three strands of embroidery thread in a contrasting colour, make neat running stitches around the bird and its wing.

### 4

Make long stitches on the tail and wing to indicate feathers, graduating them into a pleasing shape. Sew in the button eye.

### 5

With right sides facing, stitch the front and back of the sachet together, leaving a 5 cm / 2 in gap. Trim the seams. Turn it right-side out and press. Fill with dried lavender, and then slip-stitch to close the gap.

# Lacy Lavender Heart

*Evocative of the Victorian era, this exquisitely pretty heart-shaped lavender bag
is made from simple, creamy muslin, and trimmed with antique lace and
satin ribbon. The chiffon ribbon at the top is tied into a loop for hanging on
coat hangers with favourite garments.*

## MATERIALS

*paper for template
scissors
silky muslin, about
60 × 20 cm / 24 × 8 in*

*pins, needle and stranded
embroidery thread
pearl button
loose dried lavender*

*50 cm / 20 in antique lace
50 cm / 20 in very narrow
satin ribbon
50 cm / 20 in medium ribbon*

___
1

Make a heart-shaped paper template about
15 cm / 6 in high and use this as a pattern.
Cut four heart shapes from muslin. Tack
the hearts together in pairs so each heart is
a double thickness of muslin.

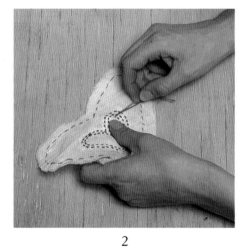

___
2

Cut a smaller heart shape from muslin.
Carefully stitch this to the centre front of one
of the larger heart shapes, using two strands
of embroidery thread and a running stitch.
Make another row of running stitches
inside this.

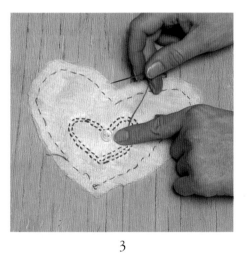

___
3

Sew the button to the top
of the smaller heart.

___
4

Stitch a third row of running stitches inside
the other two. Allow the edges of the smaller
heart to fray. With right sides facing, stitch
all around the edge of the two large double-
thickness muslin heart shapes, leaving a gap
of 5 cm / 2 in. Trim the seams, snip into
the seam at the 'V' of the heart and snip off
the bottom point within the seam allowance.
Turn the heart right-side out. Fill it with
lavender and slip-stitch to close the gap.
Don't despair if the heart looks pretty
miserable and misshapen at this stage!

**5**

Carefully slip-stitch the lace around the edge
of the heart.

**6**

Stitch the satin ribbon over the lower edge
of the lace.

**7**

Finish with a ribbon bow, arranging it so the
long tails are upwards as these can then be
joined to form a loop for hanging on
coat hangers in the wardrobe.

COUNTRY GIFTS
............................

# Herb Bath-bag

*Enjoy a traditional herbal bath by filling a fine muslin bag with relaxing herbs,
tying it to the taps and letting the hot water run through. This draw-string
design means it can be re-used time after time, if you keep refilling it with new
herbs. Chamomile and hops are relaxing; basil, and sage are invigorating.*

MATERIALS

*silky muslin, about 30 × 40 cm /
12 × 16 in
pins, needle and thread*

*scissors
fabric scraps, for casing
1 m / 39 in narrow ribbon*

*safety pin
herb bath-mix or any combination
of dried herbs*

### 1

With right sides facing, fold over about
5 cm / 2 in of the silky muslin at both short
ends, pin and stitch each side. Trim the
seams. Turn right-side out.

### 2

Turn in and hem the raw edges of the
folded-over ends.

### 3

Cut two strips of cotton fabric about
2.5 cm / 1 in wide and as long as the width
of the muslin, with about 5 mm / ¼ in extra
for turnings all round. Iron a hem along
both long edges. Turn in and hem the ends,
then pin one casing on the right side of the
muslin so the bottom edge of the casing lines
up with the hem line. Neatly stitch the
casing in place along both long seams.
Repeat with the other casing.

### 4

With right sides together, fold the muslin in
half so the casings line up. Stitch the side
seams from the bottom edge of the casing to
the bottom edge of the bag. Trim the seams.

## 5

Cut the ribbon in half, attach a safety pin to one end and use this to thread the ribbon through the casing so both ends finish up at the same side. Remove the safety pin.

## 6

Attach the safety pin to one end of the other piece of ribbon and thread it through the casing in the other direction so the ends finish up at the other side. Fill with herbs ready for use.

# Shell Pot

*Decorate a flowerpot with shells and some old netting, and then use it to hold
plants, pencils, paintbrushes, strings, ribbon, or any paraphernalia
that needs to be kept in check. It's a pretty and inexpensive way
to make a very special container.*

## MATERIALS

*small net bag
flowerpot, 18 cm / 7 in tall
scissors
hot glue gun and glue sticks
thick string
small cowrie shells
cockle shells
starfish or similar central motif*

### 1

Slip the net bag over the flowerpot and
trim the top edge. Secure it by gluing on
a length of string.

### 2

Using a glue gun, position a row of cowrie
shells along the top edge.

### 3

Glue cockle shells around the rim; position
the starfish and four cockle shells at the front.

# Shell Box

*A simple brown-paper box takes on a South-Seas feel when decorated with half-cowries. Available from craft shops, their flattened bottoms make them easy to stick to surfaces. Here, some have also been strung together to make a toggle for fastening.*

## MATERIALS

*hot glue gun and glue sticks*
*raffia*
*small buff box*
*half-cowrie shells*
*upholstery needle*

### 1

Glue a loop of raffia from the bottom of the box, up the back and along the top.

### 2

Tie half-cowries into a bunch on a length of raffia, tying each one in separately. Leave a short length of raffia free. Pierce the front of the box with an upholstery needle and thread the raffia through. Knot it on the inside.

### 3

Glue on a pattern of half-cowries to decorate the outside of the box.

# Shell Candle Centrepiece

*An old flowerpot, scallop shells gleaned from the fishmonger or kitchen and smaller shells picked up from the beach make up a fabulous, Venus-inspired table-centrepiece. Either put a candle in the centre, as here, or fill it with dried fruits or flowers.*

## MATERIALS

*hot glue gun and glue sticks
8 curved scallop shells
flowerpot, 18 cm / 7 in tall
bag of cockle shells
4 flat scallop shells
newspaper, florist's foam or
other packing material
saucer
candle
raffia*

### 1

Generously apply hot glue to the inside lower edge of a large curved scallop shell. Hold it in place on the rim of the pot for a few seconds until it is firmly stuck. Continue sticking shells to the top of the pot, arranging them so they overlap slightly, until the whole of the rim has been covered.

### 2

In the same way, glue a cockle shell where two scallops join. Continue all around the pot.

### 3

Place another row of cockles at the joins of the first row. Glue flat scallop shells face upwards to the bottom of the pot, first at the front, then at the back, and then the two sides, to ensure the pot stands straight.

### 4

Fill the pot with packing material and place a saucer on top of this. Stand a candle on the saucer.

### 5

Tie raffia around the pot where it joins the stand.

### 6

Decorate the stand with a few more cockles, if you like. Stand a few more curved scallop shells inside the original row to create a fuller, more petalled shape.

# Shell Mirror

*The subtle rose-pinks of ordinary scallop shells, picked up from the fishmonger, make for an easy, eye-catching mirror surround that's also environmentally friendly. Here, four large ones have been used at the corners with smaller ones filling in the sides.*

## MATERIALS

*sandpaper*
*mirror in wooden frame*
*paint*
*paintbrush*
*4 large flat scallop shells*
*hot glue gun and glue sticks*
*10 small flat scallop shells*
*seagrass string*
*2 metal eyelets*

1

Sand down and paint the mirror frame with the colour of your choice.

2

Position the large scallop shells at the corners of the mirror, using the hot glue.

3

In the same way, glue three of the smaller scallop shells to each side of the mirror.

4

Attach two of the smaller scallop shells to the top of the mirror and two to the bottom.

5

Plait three lengths of seagrass string to make a hanger.

6

Screw metal eyelets into each side of the frame at the back, and tie the hanger on to these.

# Chicken-wire Heart

*The garden shed provided the materials for this heart. Two shapes are simply cut
from chicken-wire and joined to give a more three-dimensional effect; then
they are decorated with string. The heart is lovely hung on the wall inside;
if it is decorated with a heavy-duty garden string it could also be hung outside.*

*newspaper for template*
*scissors*
*chicken-wire*
*wire cutters or secateurs*
*paper string or any strong string*

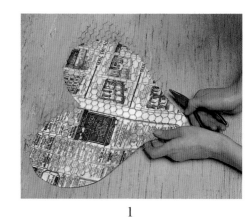

### 1

Cut a heart template about 35 cm / 14 in long
from newspaper. Use this as a pattern to cut
two heart shapes from chicken-wire.

### 2

Place one chicken-wire heart on top of the
other, and bend in the edges sharply all
round to join the shapes.

### 3

Thread strong string all around the edges
to finish, leaving two long ends free at the
centre. Thread a separate piece of string at
the centre top, and tie the ends together to
make a hanging loop.

# Raffia Heart

*This charming heart starts life, somewhat inauspiciously, as a coat hanger.
With the hook cut off, the hanger is simply bent to shape, ready to be wrapped
with raffia. A similar tiny heart, made from heavy-gauge reel wire, is hung in
the centre to finish it off.*

## MATERIALS

*wire coat hanger
wire cutters or secateurs
raffia
heavy-gauge wire*

### 1

Bend the coat hanger into a heart shape
and cut off the hook.

### 2

Starting at the base of the heart and leaving
a free length of raffia, wind raffia around the
heart to meet in the middle again. Tie the
two ends together.

### 3

Make a smaller heart from wire and bind it
with raffia. Use raffia to tie the smaller heart
so that it hangs inside the larger one.
Tie a hanging loop on to the larger heart.

# Natural Stationery

*Add your own personal style to a simple brown-paper stationery folder or notebook, by making closures from anything to hand. Here, an auger-shell and a bundle of cinnamon sticks make elegant toggles, with loops made from twine and raffia.*

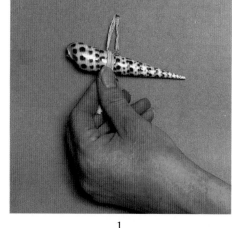

1

Work out the best position on the stationery folder or notebook for the shell or cinnamon stick toggle. Using an upholstery needle, pierce a hole in this position. Pass a loop of raffia through this to the front. Pass a short piece of raffia through this loop.

2

Tie the short piece of raffia around the shell or cinnamon stick. Secure it with a spot of glue.

3

Open the folder or notebook. Tie a knot in the raffia close to the cover. Trim the ends.

4

On the back cover, make a hole in a similar position to the one on the front cover. Thread a loop of raffia through this. Test the length by bringing it round to the front and experimenting with 'buttoning' and 'unbuttoning' the shell or stick, bearing in mind you will need extra slack to allow for knotting the loop in place. Make a knot in the raffia on the inside.

162

### 5

Close the folder or book and make another knot close to the cover on the outside so the loop is fixed firmly. Test the loop for size again, and if necessary, undo the knots and re-knot them in the right place.

### 6

Cover the knots on the insides of the covers by gluing on the small squares of brown paper to avoid damage to the adjoining pages. This is also useful if you are using material for the loop that could stain the pages, such as coloured twine or a leather thong.

COUNTRY GIFTS

# Filigree Leaf Wrap

*Even the most basic brown parcel-paper can take on a very special look. Use a gilded skeletonized leaf and gold twine in combination with brown paper: chunky coir string would give a more robust look.*

## MATERIALS

*picture framer's wax gilt
large skeletonized leaf
brown paper
sticky tape
gold twine
hot glue gun and glue sticks,
if necessary*

**1**

Rub wax gilt into the skeletonized leaf.

**2**

Wrap the parcel in the brown paper and rub gilt wax on to the corners. Tie the parcel with gold twine, bringing the two ends together and tying a knot. Fray the ends to create a tassle effect. Slip the leaf under the twine, securing it with glue at each end if necessary.

# Fruit and Foliage Gift-wraps

*Here, gilded brown parcel-paper provides a fitting background for a decoration of leaves and dried fruit slices.*

## MATERIALS

*brown paper
sticky tape
picture framer's wax gilt
seagrass string
hot glue gun and glue sticks
dried fruit slices
preserved leaves*

**1**

Wrap the parcel with brown paper and rub in gilt wax, paying special attention to the corners.

**2**

Tie the parcel with seagrass string, and then glue a different dried fruit or leaf to each quarter.

164

# Tissue Rosette Gift-wrap

*Tissue papers make a fabulous foundation for any gift-wrapping; they come in a glorious array of colours, and they softly take to any shape.*

*tissue paper in 2 shades
co-ordinating twine*

### 1

Place a cylindrical gift in the centre of two squares of tissue, one laid on top of the other. Gather the tissue up and tie it with twine.

### 2

Gently open out the rosette at the top.

# Lavender Tissue Gift-wrap

*Bunches of lavender add a real country touch to tissue gift-wrap, and become part of the gift.*

*dried lavender
twine
tissue paper in 2 shades
sticky tape
glue*

### 1

Make two bunches of lavender and tie them with twine to form a cross.

### 2

Wrap the parcel in the darker toned tissue paper, and then wrap it with the paler tissue, cut to form an envelope. Glue the lavender to the front of the parcel.

# Bath-time Bottle

*Recycle a glass bottle containing home-made lotion and decorate it with corrugated card in gem-like colours for a real impact.*

### MATERIALS

*scissors*
*coloured corrugated card*
*flower-water bottle*
*hot glue gun and glue sticks*
*coloured raffia*

___1___

Cut the corrugated card to size, and then glue in position around the bottle. Tie with raffia.

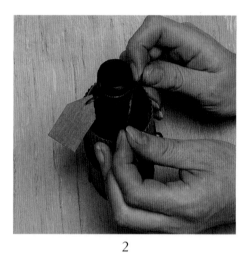

___2___

Make a matching label from corrugated card, and tie it on using raffia.

# Bath-time Treat Jar

*Decorate a jar of lotion to complement the bottle, using brilliantly coloured fine corrugated card. Royal blue and emerald green make a rich combination that could be used for both men and women.*

### MATERIALS

*scissors*
*coloured corrugated card*
*baby-food jar*
*hot glue gun and glue sticks*
*twine*

___1___

Cut the corrugated card to size, and then glue in place around the jar. Tie the twine around the jar.

___2___

Cut a piece of corrugated card to fit the top of the lid and glue it in place. Glue twine to cover the side of the lid.

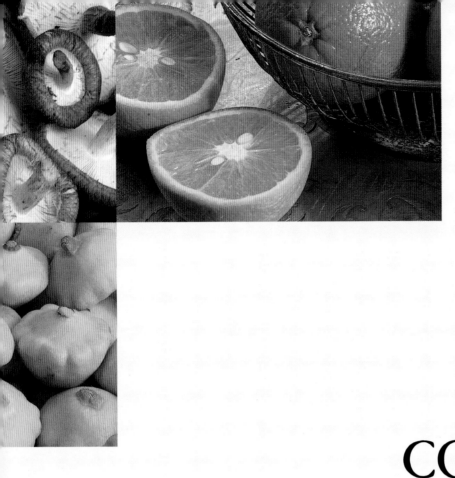

# COUNTRY
# Cooking

## LIZ TRIGG

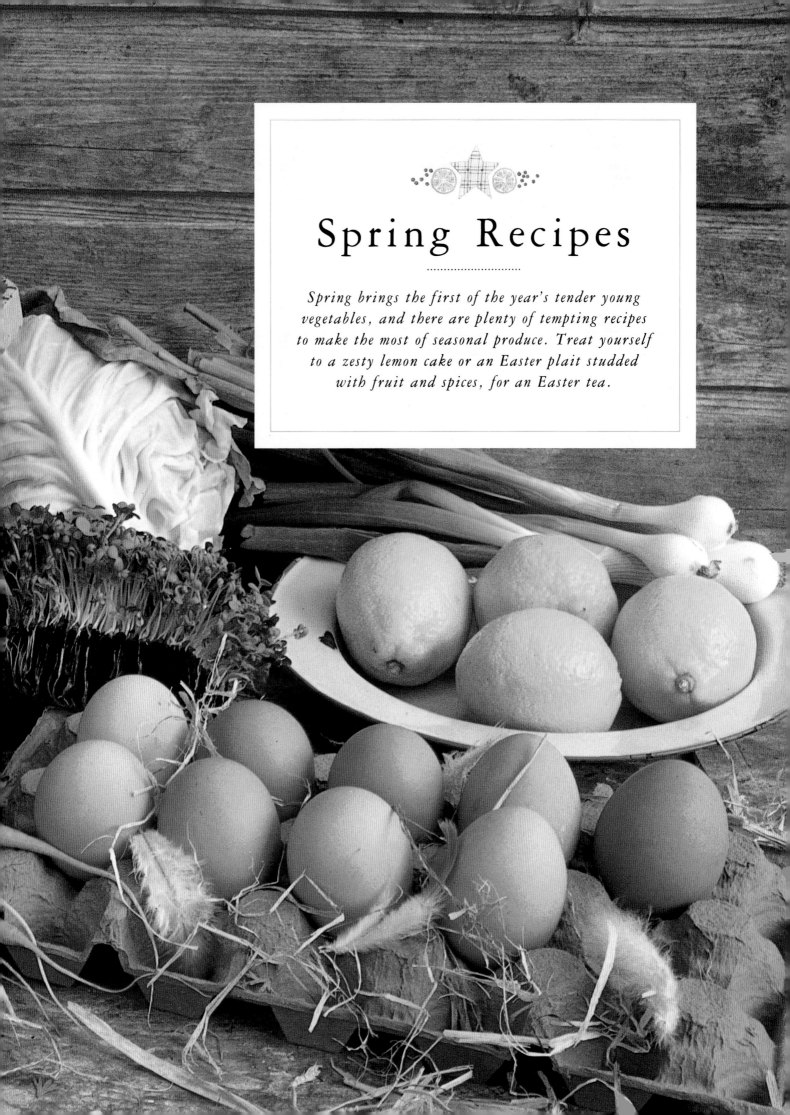

# Spring Recipes

Spring brings the first of the year's tender young vegetables, and there are plenty of tempting recipes to make the most of seasonal produce. Treat yourself to a zesty lemon cake or an Easter plait studded with fruit and spices, for an Easter tea.

# Spring Roasted Chicken with Fresh Herbs and Garlic

*A smaller chicken or four poussins can also be roasted in this way.*

### INGREDIENTS

*1.75 kg / 4½ lb free-range chicken
or 4 small poussins
finely grated rind and
juice of 1 lemon
1 garlic clove, crushed
30 ml / 2 tbsp olive oil
2 fresh thyme sprigs
2 fresh sage sprigs
75 g / 3 oz / 6 tbsp unsalted butter,
softened
salt and freshly ground
black pepper*

**Serves 4**

1

Season the chicken or poussins well.
Mix the lemon rind and juice, garlic and
olive oil together and pour them over the
chicken. Leave to marinate for at least
2 hours in a non-metallic dish.
When the chicken has marinated preheat
the oven to 230°C / 450°F / Gas Mark 8.

2

Place the herbs in the cavity of the bird and
smear the butter over the skin. Season well.
Roast the chicken for 10 minutes, then turn
the oven down to 190°C / 375°F / Gas Mark 5.
Baste the chicken well, and then roast for a
further 1 hour 30 minutes, until the juices run
clear when the thigh is pierced with a skewer.
Leave to rest for 15 minutes before carving.

# Lemon and Rosemary Lamb Chops

*Spring lamb is delicious with the fresh flavour of lemon. Garnish with sprigs of
fresh rosemary – the aroma is irresistible.*

### INGREDIENTS

*12 lamb cutlets
45 ml / 3 tbsp olive oil
2 large rosemary sprigs
juice of 1 lemon
3 garlic cloves, sliced
salt and freshly ground
black pepper*

**Serves 4**

1

Trim the excess fat from the cutlets.
Mix the oil, rosemary, lemon juice and
garlic together and season well.

2

Pour over the chops in a shallow dish and
marinate for 30 minutes. Remove from the
marinade, and blot the excess with kitchen
paper and grill for 10 minutes on each side.

# Carrot and Coriander Soufflés

*Use tender young carrots for this light-as-air dish.*

INGREDIENTS

*450 g / 1 lb carrots*
*30 ml / 2 tbsp fresh chopped*
*coriander*
*4 eggs, separated*
*salt and freshly ground*
*black pepper*

**Serves 4**

1

Peel the carrots.

2

Cook in boiling salted water for 20 minutes or until tender. Drain, and process until smooth in a food processor.

3

Preheat the oven to 200°C / 400°F / Gas Mark 6. Season the puréed carrots well, and stir in the chopped coriander.

4

Fold the egg yolks into the carrot mixture.

5

In a separate bowl, whisk the egg whites until stiff.

6

Fold the egg whites into the carrot mixture and pour into four greased ramekins. Bake for about 20 minutes or until risen and golden. Serve immediately.

# Leeks with Ham and Cheese Sauce

*A tasty teatime or supper dish: use a strong cheese for best results.*

### INGREDIENTS

*4 leeks*
*4 slices ham*

For the sauce
*25 g / 1 oz / 2 tbsp unsalted butter*
*25 g / 1 oz / 1 tbsp plain flour*
*300 ml / ½ pint / 1¼ cups milk*
*½ tsp French mustard*
*115 g / 4 oz hard cheese, grated*
*salt and freshly ground*
*black pepper*

**Serves 4**

**1**

Preheat the oven to 190°C / 375°F /
Gas Mark 5. Trim the leeks to 2 cm / 1 in of
the white and cook in salted water for about
20 minutes until soft. Drain thoroughly.
Wrap the leeks in the ham slices.

**2**

To make the sauce, melt the butter in a
saucepan. Add the flour and cook for a few
minutes. Remove from the heat and
gradually add the milk, whisking well with
each addition. Return to the heat and whisk
until the sauce thickens. Stir in the mustard
and 75 g / 3 oz of the cheese and season well.
Lay the leeks in a shallow ovenproof dish and
pour over the sauce. Scatter the extra cheese
on top and bake for 20 minutes.

# Baked Eggs with Double Cream and Chives

*This is a rich dish best served with Melba toast: it's very easy and quick to make.*

### INGREDIENTS

*15 g / ½ oz / 1 tbsp unsalted*
*butter, softened*
*60 ml / 4 tbsp double cream*
*15 ml / 1 tbsp snipped fresh chives*
*4 eggs*
*50 g / 2 oz Gruyère cheese,*
*finely grated*
*salt and freshly ground*
*black pepper*

**Serves 2**

**1**

Preheat the oven to 180°C / 350°F /
Gas Mark 4. Grease two individual gratin
dishes. Mix the cream with the chives,
and season with salt and pepper.

**2**

Break the eggs into each dish and top with
the cream mixture. Sprinkle the cheese
around the edges of the dishes and bake in
the oven for 15–20 minutes. When cooked,
brown the tops under the grill for a minute.

# Lemon Drizzle Cake

*You can also make this recipe using a large orange instead of the lemons; either way, it makes a zesty treat for afternoon tea.*

### INGREDIENTS

*finely grated rind of 2 lemons*
*175 g / 6 oz / 12 tbsp caster sugar*
*225 g / 8 oz / 1 cup unsalted
butter, softened*
*4 eggs*
*225 g / 8 oz / 2 cups self-raising
flour*
*5 ml / 1 tsp baking powder*
*¼ tsp salt*
*shredded rind of 1 lemon,
to decorate*

For the syrup
*juice of 1 lemon*
*150 g / 5 oz / ¾ cup caster sugar*

**Serves 6**

### 1

Preheat the oven to 160°C / 325°F /
Gas Mark 3. Grease a 1 kg / 2 lb loaf tin or
18–20 cm / 7–8 in round cake tin and line it
with greaseproof paper or baking parchment.
Mix the lemon rind and caster sugar together.

### 2

Cream the butter with the lemon and sugar
mixture. Add the eggs and mix until
smooth. Sift the flour, baking powder and
salt into a bowl and fold a third at a time into
the mixture. Turn the batter into the tin,
smooth the top and bake for 1½ hours or
until golden brown and springy to the touch.

### 3

To make the syrup, slowly heat the juice
with the sugar and dissolve it gently. Make
several slashes in the top of the cake and pour
over the syrup. Sprinkle the shredded lemon
rind and 5 ml / 1 tsp granulated sugar on top
and leave to cool.

# Wholemeal Bread

*Home-made bread creates one of the most evocative smells in country cooking.*
*Eat this on the day of making, to enjoy the superb fresh taste.*

### INGREDIENTS

20 g / ¾ oz fresh yeast
300 ml / ½ pint / 1 ¼ cups
lukewarm milk
5 ml / 1 tsp caster sugar
225 g / 8 oz / 1 ½ cups strong
wholemeal flour, sifted
225 g / 8 oz / 2 cups strong
white flour, sifted
5 ml / 1 tsp salt
50 g / 2 oz / 4 tbsp butter,
chilled and cubed
1 egg, lightly beaten
30 ml / 2 tbsp mixed seeds

**Makes 4 rounds or 2 loaves**

**1**

Gently dissolve the yeast with a little of the milk and the sugar to make a paste. Place both the flours plus any bran from the sieve and the salt in a large warmed mixing bowl. Rub in the butter until the mixture resembles breadcrumbs.

**2**

Add the yeast mixture, remaining milk and egg and mix into a fairly soft dough. Knead on a floured board for 15 minutes. Lightly grease the mixing bowl and put the dough back in the bowl, covering it with a piece of greased cling film. Leave to double in size in a warm place (this should take at least an hour).

**3**

Knock the dough back and knead it for a further 10 minutes. Preheat the oven to 200°C / 400°F / Gas Mark 6. To make round loaves, divide the dough into four pieces and shape them into flattish rounds. Place them on a floured baking sheet and leave to rise for a further 15 minutes. Sprinkle the loaves with the mixed seeds. Bake for about 20 minutes until golden and firm.

NOTE

For tin-shaped loaves, put the knocked-back dough into two greased loaf tins instead. Leave to rise for a further 45 minutes and then bake for about 45 minutes, until the loaf sounds hollow when turned out of the tin and knocked on the base.

# Easter Plait

*Serve this delicious plait sliced with butter and jam.*
*It is also very good toasted on the day after you made it.*

### INGREDIENTS

200 ml / 7 fl oz / ⅞ cup milk
2 eggs, lightly beaten
450 g / 1 lb / 4 cups plain flour
½ tsp salt
10 ml / 2 tsp ground mixed spice
75 g / 3 oz / 6 tbsp butter
20 g / ¾ oz dried yeast
75 g / 3 oz / 6 tbsp caster sugar

175 g / 6 oz / 1¼ cups currants
25 g / 1 oz / ¼ cup candied mixed
peel, chopped
a little sweetened milk, to glaze
25 g / 1 oz / 1½ tbsp glacé
cherries, chopped
15 g / ½ oz / 1 tbsp angelica,
chopped

**Serves 8**

### 1

Warm the milk to lukewarm, add two-thirds of it to the eggs and mix well.

### 2

Sift the flour, salt and mixed spice together. Rub in the butter, then add the sugar and dried yeast. Make a well in the centre, and add the milk mixture, adding more milk as necessary to make a sticky dough.

### 3

Knead on a well-floured surface and then knead in the currants and mixed peel, reserving 15 ml / 1 tbsp for the topping. Put the dough in a lightly greased bowl and cover it with a damp tea towel. Leave to double its size. Preheat the oven to 220°C / 425°F / Gas Mark 7.

### 4

Turn the dough out on to a floured surface and knead again for 2–3 minutes. Divide the dough into three even pieces. Roll each piece into a sausage shape roughly 20 cm / 8 in long. Plait the three pieces together, turning under and pinching each end. Place on a floured baking sheet and leave to rise for 15 minutes.

### 5

Brush the top with sweetened milk and scatter with roughly chopped cherries, strips of angelica and the reserved mixed peel. Bake in the preheated oven for 45 minutes or until the bread sounds hollow when tapped on the bottom. Cool slightly on a wire rack.

# Orange-blossom Jelly

*A fresh orange jelly makes a delightful dessert: the natural fruit flavour combined with the smooth jelly has a cleansing quality that is especially welcome after a rich main course. This is delicious served with thin, crisp* langues de chat *biscuits.*

## INGREDIENTS

*65 g / 2½ oz / 5 tbsp caster sugar*
*150 ml / ¼ pint / ⅔ cup water*
*2 sachets of gelatine*
*(about 25 g / 1 oz)*
*600 ml / 1 pint / 2½ cups freshly squeezed orange juice*
*30 ml / 2 tbsp orange-flower water*

**Serves 4–6**

### 1

Place the caster sugar and water in a small saucepan and gently heat to dissolve the sugar. Leave to cool.

### 2

Sprinkle over the gelatine, ensuring it is completely submerged in the water. Leave to stand until the gelatine has absorbed all the liquid and is solid.

### 3

Gently melt the gelatine over a bowl of simmering water until it becomes clear and transparent. Leave to cool. When the gelatine is cold, mix it with the orange juice and orange-flower water.

### 4

Wet a jelly mould and pour in the jelly. Chill in the refrigerator for at least 2 hours, or until set. Turn out to serve.

# Rhubarb and Orange Crumble

*The almonds give this crumble topping a nutty taste and crunchy texture.*
*This crumble is extra-delicious with home-made custard.*

INGREDIENTS

900 g / 2 lb rhubarb, cut in
5 cm / 2 in lengths
75 g / 3 oz / 6 tbsp caster sugar
finely grated rind and juice
of 2 oranges

115 g / 4 oz / 1 cup plain flour
115 g / 4 oz / ½ cup unsalted
butter, chilled and cubed
75 g / 3 oz / 6 tbsp demerara sugar
115 g / 4 oz / 1¼ cups ground almonds

**Serves 6**

### 1

Preheat the oven to 180°C / 350°F /
Gas Mark 4. Place the rhubarb in a shallow
ovenproof dish.

### 2

Sprinkle over the caster sugar and add the
orange rind and juice.

### 3

Sift the flour into a mixing bowl and add the
butter. Rub the butter into the flour until
the mixture resembles breadcrumbs.

### 4

Add the demerara sugar and ground almonds
and mix well.

### 5

Spoon the crumble mixture over the fruit to
cover it completely. Bake for 40 minutes,
until the top is browned and the fruit is
cooked. Serve warm.

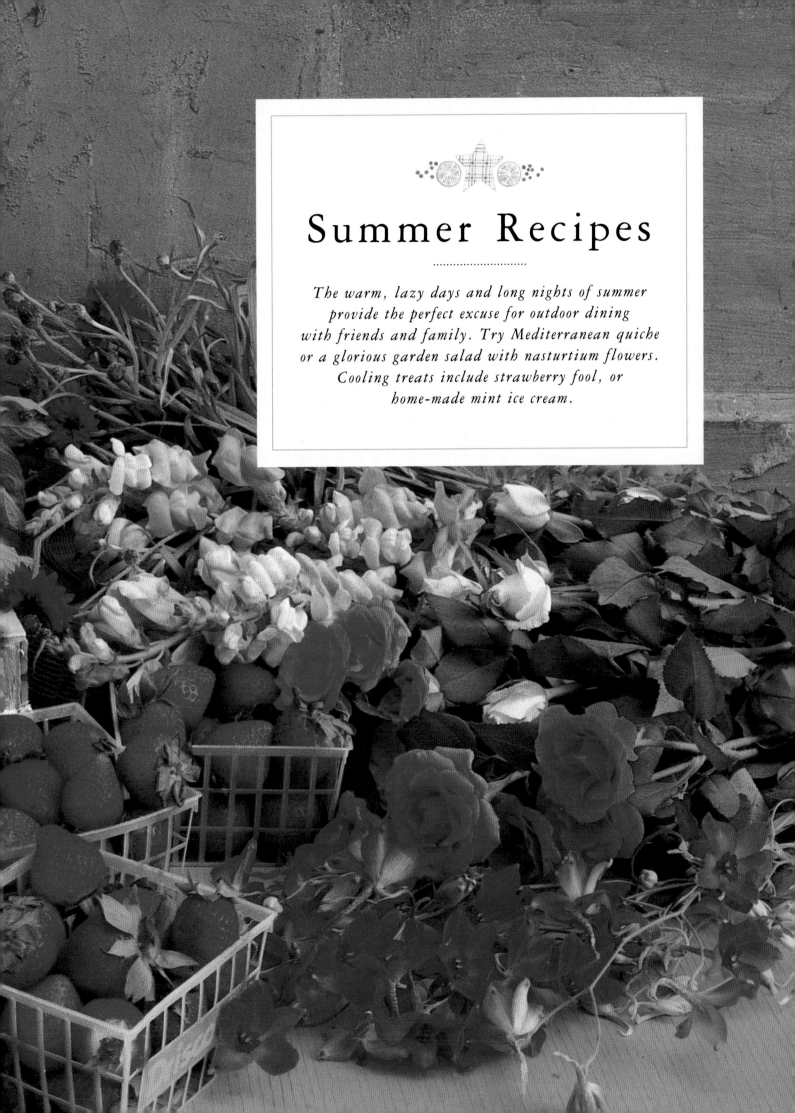

# Summer Recipes

..........................

*The warm, lazy days and long nights of summer
provide the perfect excuse for outdoor dining
with friends and family. Try Mediterranean quiche
or a glorious garden salad with nasturtium flowers.
Cooling treats include strawberry fool, or
home-made mint ice cream.*

# Mackerel with Roasted Blueberries

*Fresh blueberries burst with flavour when roasted, and their sharpness*
*complements the rich flesh of mackerel very well.*

### INGREDIENTS

*15 g / ½ oz / 2 tsp plain flour*
*4 small cooked, smoked mackerel*
*fillets*
*50 g / 2 oz / 4 tbsp unsalted butter*
*juice of ½ lemon*
*salt and freshly ground*
*black pepper*

For the roasted blueberries
*450 g / 1 lb blueberries*
*25 g / 1 oz / 2 tbsp caster sugar*
*15 g / ½ oz / 1 tbsp unsalted butter*
*salt and freshly ground*
*black pepper*

**Serves 4**

1

Preheat the oven to 200°C / 400°F /
Gas Mark 6. Season the flour. Dip each fish
fillet into the flour to coat it well.

2

Dot the butter on the fillets and bake in the
oven for 20 minutes.

3

Place the blueberries, sugar, butter and
seasoning in a separate small roasting tin
and roast them, basting them occasionally,
for 15 minutes. To serve, drizzle the
lemon juice over the roasted mackerel,
accompanied by the roasted blueberries.

# Griddled Trout with Bacon

*This dish can also be cooked on the barbecue.*

### INGREDIENTS

*25 g / 1 oz / 1 tbsp plain flour*
*4 trout, cleaned and gutted*
*75 g / 3 oz streaky bacon*
*50 g / 2 oz / 4 tbsp butter*
*15 ml / 1 tbsp olive oil*
*juice of ½ lemon*
*salt and freshly ground*
*black pepper*

**Serves 4**

1

Pat the trout dry with kitchen roll and
mix the flour and seasoning together.

2

Roll the trout in the seasoned flour mixture
and wrap tightly in the streaky bacon.
Heat a heavy frying pan. Heat the butter and
oil in the pan and fry the trout for 5 minutes
on each side. Serve immediately, with the
lemon juice drizzled on top.

# Mediterranean Quiche

*The strong Mediterranean flavours of tomatoes, peppers and anchovies*
*complement beautifully the cheesy pastry in this unusual quiche.*

### INGREDIENTS

For the pastry
*225 g / 8 oz / 2 cups plain flour*
*pinch of salt*
*pinch of dry mustard*
*115 g / 4 oz / ½ cup butter,*
*chilled and cubed*
*50 g / 2 oz Gruyère cheese, grated*

For the filling
*50 g / 2 oz can of anchovies in oil,*
*drained*
*50 ml / 2 fl oz / ¼ cup milk*
*30 ml / 2 tbsp French mustard*
*45 ml / 3 tbsp olive oil*
*2 large Spanish onions, sliced*
*1 red pepper, seeded and*
*very finely sliced*
*3 egg yolks*
*350 ml / 12 fl oz / 1½ cups*
*double cream*
*1 garlic clove, crushed*
*175 g / 6 oz mature Cheddar*
*cheese, grated*
*2 large tomatoes, thickly sliced*
*salt and freshly ground*
*black pepper*
*30 ml / 2 tbsp chopped fresh basil,*
*to garnish*

**Serves 12**

__1__

First make the pastry. Place the flour, salt
and mustard powder in a food processor,
add the butter and process the mixture
until it resembles breadcrumbs.

__2__

Add the cheese and process again briefly.
Add enough iced water to make a stiff dough:
it will be ready when the dough forms a ball.
Wrap with cling film and chill for 30 minutes.

__3__

Meanwhile, make the filling. Soak the
anchovies in the milk for 20 minutes.
Drain away the milk.

__4__

Roll out the chilled pastry and line a 23 cm /
9 in loose-based flan tin. Spread over the
mustard and chill for a further 15 minutes.

__5__

Preheat the oven to 200°C / 400°F /
Gas Mark 6. Heat the oil in a frying pan and
cook the onions and red pepper until soft.
In a separate bowl, beat the egg yolks,
cream, garlic and Cheddar cheese together;
season well. Arrange the tomatoes in a
single layer in the pastry case. Top with the
onion and pepper mixture and the anchovy
fillets. Pour over the egg mixture.
Bake for 30–35 minutes. Sprinkle over
the basil and serve.

# New Potato Salad

*Potatoes freshly dug up from the garden are the best. Always leave the skins on: just wash the dirt away thoroughly. If you add the mayonnaise and other ingredients when the potatoes are hot, the flavours will develop as the potatoes cool.*

## INGREDIENTS

*900 g / 2 lb baby new potatoes*
*2 green apples, cored and chopped*
*4 spring onions, chopped*
*3 celery sticks, finely chopped*
*150 ml / ¼ pint / ⅔ cup*
*mayonnaise*
*salt and freshly ground*
*black pepper*

**Serves 6**

1

Cook the potatoes in salted, boiling water for about 20 minutes, or until they are very tender.

2

Drain the potatoes well and immediately add the remaining ingredients and stir until well mixed. Leave to cool and serve cold.

# French Bean Salad

*The secret of this recipe is to dress the beans while still hot.*

## INGREDIENTS

*175 g / 6 oz cherry tomatoes,*
*halved*
*5 ml / 1 tsp sugar*
*450 g / 1 lb French beans,*
*topped and tailed*
*175 g / 6 oz feta cheese, cubed*
*salt and freshly ground*
*black pepper*

For the dressing
*90 ml / 6 tbsp olive oil*
*45 ml / 3 tbsp white-wine vinegar*
*¼ tsp Dijon mustard*
*2 garlic cloves, crushed*
*salt and freshly ground*
*black pepper*

**Serves 6**

1

Preheat the oven to 230°C / 450°F / Gas Mark 8. Put the cherry tomatoes on a baking sheet and sprinkle over the sugar, salt and pepper. Roast for 20 minutes, then leave to cool. Meanwhile, cook the beans in boiling, salted water for 10 minutes.

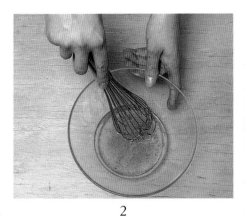

2

Make the dressing by whisking together the oil, vinegar, mustard, garlic and seasoning. Drain the beans and immediately pour over the vinaigrette and mix well. When cool, stir in the roasted tomatoes and the feta cheese. Serve chilled.

# Squash à la Greque

*A traditional French-style dish that is usually made with mushrooms.
Make sure that you cook the baby squash until they are quite tender,
so they can fully absorb the delicious flavours of the marinade.*

## INGREDIENTS

*175 g / 6 oz patty-pan squash
250 ml / 8 fl oz / 1 cup white wine
juice of 2 lemons
fresh thyme sprig
bay leaf
small bunch of fresh chervil,
roughly chopped
1/4 tsp coriander seeds, crushed
1/4 tsp black peppercorns, crushed
75 ml / 5 tbsp olive oil*

**Serves 4**

1

Blanch the patty-pan squash in boiling
water for 3 minutes, and then refresh them
in cold water.

2

Place all the remaining ingredients in a pan,
add 150 ml / 1/2 pint / 2/3 cup of water and
simmer for 10 minutes, covered. Add the
patty-pans and cook for 10 minutes. Remove
with a slotted spoon when they are cooked
and tender to the bite.

3

Reduce the liquid by boiling hard for
10 minutes. Strain it and pour it over the
squashes. Leave until cool for the flavours to
be absorbed. Serve cold.

# Garden Salad

*You can use any fresh, edible flowers from your garden for this beautiful salad.*

## INGREDIENTS

*1 cos lettuce*
*175 g / 6 oz rocket*
*1 small frisée lettuce*
*fresh chervil and tarragon sprigs*
*15 ml / 1 tbsp snipped fresh chives*
*handful of mixed edible flower*
*heads, such as nasturtiums*
*or marigolds*

*For the dressing*
*45 ml / 3 tbsp olive oil*
*15 ml / 1 tbsp white-wine vinegar*
*½ tsp French mustard*
*1 garlic clove, crushed*
*pinch of sugar*

**Serves 4**

**1**

Mix the cos, rocket and frisée leaves
and herbs together.

**2**

Make the dressing by whisking all the
ingredients together in a large bowl. Toss the
salad leaves in the bowl with the dressing,
add the flower heads and serve at once.

# Country Strawberry Fool

*Make this delicious fool on the day you want to eat it, and chill it well,
for the best strawberry taste.*

## INGREDIENTS

*300 ml / ½ pint / 1¼ cups milk*
*2 egg yolks*
*90 g / 3½ oz / scant ½ cup
caster sugar*
*few drops of vanilla essence*
*900 g / 2 lb ripe strawberries*
*juice of ½ lemon*
*300 ml / ½ pint / 1¼ cups double
cream*

To decorate
*12 small strawberries*
*4 fresh mint sprigs*

**Serves 4**

1

First make the custard. Whisk 30 ml / 2 tbsp
milk with the egg yolks, 15 ml / 1 tbsp caster
sugar and the vanilla essence.

2

Heat the remaining milk until it is just
below boiling point.

3

Stir the milk into the egg mixture. Rinse
the pan out and return the mixture to it.

4

Gently heat and whisk until the mixture
thickens (it should be thick enough to coat
the back of a spoon). Lay a wet piece of
greaseproof paper on top of the custard and
leave it to cool.

5

Purée the strawberries in a food processor or
blender with the lemon juice and the
remaining sugar.

6

Lightly whip the cream and fold in the fruit
purée and custard. Pour into glass dishes and
decorate with the whole strawberries and
sprigs of mint.

# Mint Ice Cream

*This ice cream is best served slightly softened, so take it out*
*of the freezer 20 minutes before you want to serve it. For a special occasion,*
*this looks spectacular served in an ice bowl.*

## INGREDIENTS

*8 egg yolks*
*75 g / 3 oz / 6 tbsp caster sugar*
*600 ml / 1 pint / 2½ cups single*
*cream*
*1 vanilla pod*
*60 ml / 4 tbsp chopped fresh mint*

**Serves 8**

### 1

Beat the egg yolks and sugar until they are
pale and light using a hand-held electric
beater or a balloon whisk. Transfer to a
small saucepan.

### 2

In a separate saucepan, bring the cream to
the boil with the vanilla pod.

### 3

Remove the vanilla pod and pour the hot cream
on to the egg mixture, whisking briskly.

### 4

Continue whisking to ensure the eggs
are mixed into the cream.

### 5

Gently heat the mixture until the custard
thickens enough to coat the back of a
wooden spoon. Leave to cool.

### 6

Stir in the mint and place in an ice-cream
maker to churn, about 3–4 hours. If you
don't have an ice-cream maker, freeze the
ice cream until mushy and then whisk it well
again, to break down the ice crystals. Freeze
for another 3 hours until it is softly frozen
and whisk again. Finally freeze until hard:
at least 6 hours.

# Mixed Berry Tart

*The orange-flavoured pastry is delicious with the fresh fruits of summer.*
*Serve this with some extra shreds of orange rind scattered on top.*

### INGREDIENTS

**For the pastry**
*225 g / 8 oz / 2 cups plain flour*
*115 g / 4 oz / ½ cup unsalted*
*butter*
*finely grated rind of 1 orange,*
*plus extra to decorate*

**For the filling**
*300 ml / ½ pint / 1¼ cups*
*crème fraîche*
*finely grated rind of 1 lemon*
*10 ml / 2 tsp icing sugar*
*675 g / 1½ lb mixed*
*summer berries*

**Serves 8**

**1**

To make the pastry, put the flour and butter in a large bowl. Rub in the butter until the mixture resembles breadcrumbs.

**2**

Add the orange rind and enough cold water to make a soft dough.

**3**

Roll into a ball and chill for at least 30 minutes. Roll out the pastry on a lightly floured surface.

**4**

Line a 23 cm / 9 in loose-based flan tin with the pastry. Chill for 30 minutes. Preheat the oven to 200°C / 400°F / Gas Mark 6 and place a baking sheet in the oven to heat up. Line the tin with greaseproof paper and baking beans and bake blind on the baking sheet for 15 minutes. Remove the paper and beans and bake for 10 minutes more, until the pastry is golden. Allow to cool completely. To make the filling, whisk the crème fraîche, lemon rind and sugar together and pour into the pastry case. Top with fruit, sprinkle with orange rind and serve sliced.

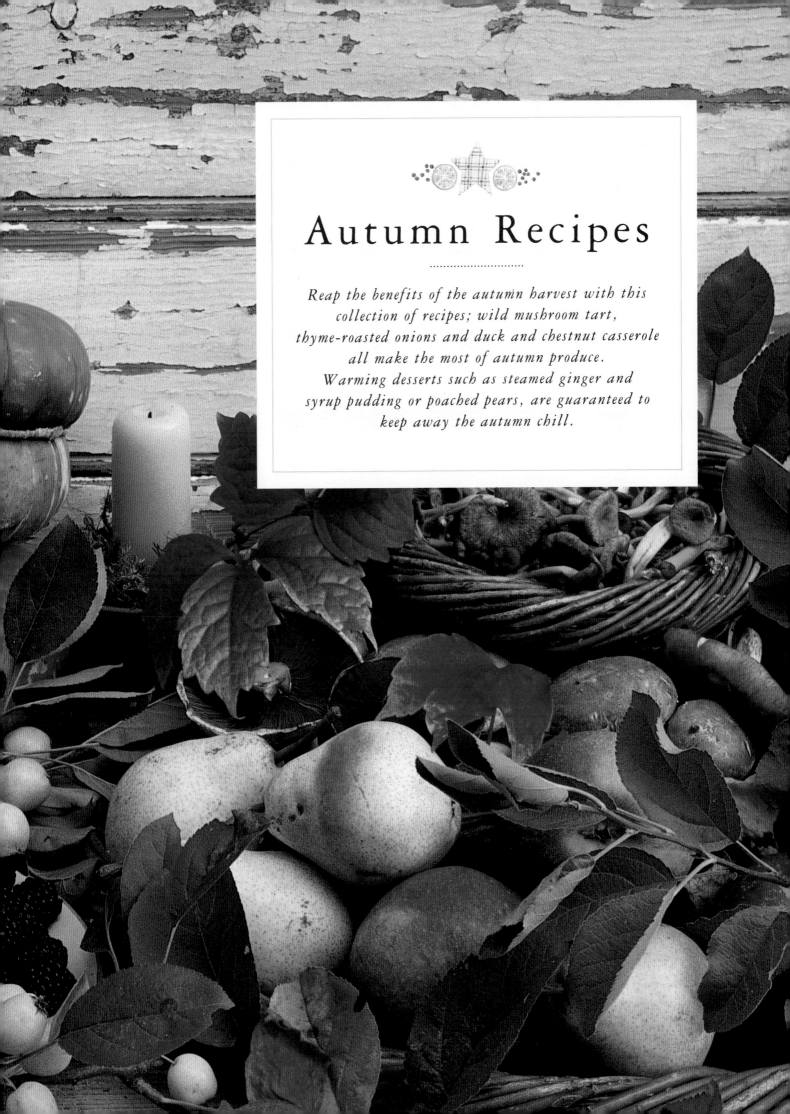

# Autumn Recipes

*Reap the benefits of the autumn harvest with this
collection of recipes; wild mushroom tart,
thyme-roasted onions and duck and chestnut casserole
all make the most of autumn produce.
Warming desserts such as steamed ginger and
syrup pudding or poached pears, are guaranteed to
keep away the autumn chill.*

# Wild Mushroom Tart

*The flavour of wild mushrooms makes this tart really rich: use as wide a variety of mushrooms as you can get.*

## INGREDIENTS

**For the pastry**
225 g / 8 oz / 2 cups plain flour
50 g / 2 oz / 4 tbsp hard white fat
10 ml / 2 tsp lemon juice
about 150 ml / ¼ pint / ⅔ cup
ice-cold water
115 g / 4 oz / ½ cup butter,
chilled and cubed
1 egg, beaten, to glaze

**For the filling**
150 g / 5 oz / 10 tbsp butter
2 shallots, finely chopped
2 garlic cloves, crushed
450 g / 1 lb mixed wild
mushrooms, sliced
45 ml / 3 tbsp chopped fresh parsley
30 ml / 2 tbsp double cream
salt and freshly ground
black pepper

**Serves 6**

### 1

To make the pastry, sieve the flour and
½ tsp salt together into a large bowl.
Add the white fat and rub into the mixture
until it resembles breadcrumbs.

### 2

Add the lemon juice and enough iced water
to make a soft but not sticky dough.
Cover and chill for 20 minutes.

### 3

Roll the pastry out into a rectangle on a
lightly floured surface. Mark the dough into
three equal strips and arrange half the butter
cubes over two-thirds of the dough.

### 5

Chill the pastry for 20 minutes. Repeat the
process of marking into thirds, folding over,
giving a quarter turn and rolling out three
times, chilling for 20 minutes in between
each time. To make the filling, melt
50 g / 2 oz / 4 tbsp butter and fry the shallots
and garlic until soft but not browned. Add
the remaining butter and the mushrooms
and cook for 35–40 minutes. Drain off any
excess liquid and stir in the remaining
ingredients. Leave to cool. Preheat the oven
to 220°C / 450°F / Gas Mark 7.

### 4

Fold the outer two-thirds over, folding over
the uncovered third last. Seal the edges with
a rolling pin. Give the dough a quarter turn
and roll it out again. Mark it into thirds and
dot with the remaining butter cubes
in the same way.

### 6

Divide the pastry in two. Roll out one half
into a 22 cm / 9 in round, cutting around a
plate to make a neat shape. Pile the filling
into the centre. Roll out the remaining
pastry large enough to cover the base. Brush
the edges of the base with water and then lay
the second pastry circle on top. Press the
edges together to seal and brush the top with
a little beaten egg. Bake for 45 minutes,
or until the pastry is risen, golden and flaky.

# Mushroom and Parsley Soup

*Thickened with bread, this rich mushroom soup will warm you up
on cold autumn days. It makes a terrific hearty lunch.*

### INGREDIENTS

*75 g / 3 oz / 6 tbsp unsalted butter*
*900 g / 2 lb field mushrooms,
sliced*
*2 onions, roughly chopped*
*600 ml / 1 pint / 2½ cups milk*
*8 slices white bread*
*60 ml / 4 tbsp chopped fresh parsley*
*300 ml / ½ pint / 1¼ cups
double cream*
*salt and freshly ground
black pepper*

**Serves 8**

1

Melt the butter and sauté the mushrooms
and onions until soft but not coloured –
about 10 minutes. Add the milk.

2

Tear the bread into pieces, drop them into
the soup and leave the bread to soak for
15 minutes. Purée the soup and return it to
the pan. Add the parsley, cream and seasoning.
Re-heat, but do not allow the soup to boil.
Serve at once.

# Thyme-roasted Onions

*These slowly roasted onions develop a delicious, sweet flavour which is perfect
with roast meat. You could prepare par-boiled new potatoes in the same way.*

### INGREDIENTS

*75 ml / 5 tbsp olive oil*
*50 g / 2 oz / 4 tbsp unsalted butter*
*900 g / 2 lb small onions*
*30 ml / 2 tbsp chopped fresh thyme*
*salt and freshly ground
black pepper*

**Serves 4**

1

Preheat the oven to 220°C / 425°F /
Gas Mark 7. Heat the oil and butter in a
large roasting tin. Add the onions and toss
them in the oil and butter mixture.

2

Add the thyme and seasoning and roast for
45 minutes, basting regularly.

# Duck and Chestnut Casserole

*Serve this casserole with a mixture of mashed potatoes and celeriac,
to soak up the rich duck juices.*

### INGREDIENTS

*1.75 kg / 4½ lb duck*
*45 ml / 3 tbsp olive oil*
*175 g / 6 oz small onions*
*50 g / 2 oz field mushrooms*
*50 g / 2 oz shiitake mushrooms*
*300 ml / ½ pint / 1¼ cups
red wine*
*300 ml / ½ pint / 1¼ cups
beef stock*
*225 g / 8 oz canned, peeled,
unsweetened chestnuts, drained
salt and freshly ground
black pepper*

**Serves 4–6**

1

Joint the duck into eight pieces. Heat the oil
in a large frying pan and brown the duck
pieces. Remove from the frying pan.

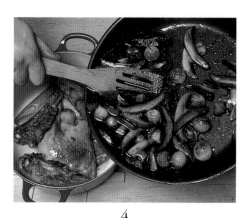

2

Add the onions to the pan and brown them
well for 10 minutes.

3

Add the mushrooms and cook for a few
minutes more. Deglaze the pan with the
red wine and boil to reduce the volume
by half. Meanwhile, preheat the oven to
180°C / 350°F / Gas Mark 4.

4

Pour the wine and the stock into a
casserole. Replace the duck, add the
chestnuts, season well and cook in the oven
for 1½ hours.

# Cheese Scones

*These delicious scones make a good tea-time treat. They are best served fresh and still slightly warm.*

### INGREDIENTS

*225 g / 8 oz / 2 cups plain flour*
*12 ml / 2½ tsp baking powder*
*½ tsp dry mustard powder*
*½ tsp salt*
*50 g / 2 oz / 4 tbsp butter, chilled*
*75 g / 3 oz Cheddar cheese, grated*
*150 ml / ¼ pint / ⅔ cup milk*
*1 egg, beaten*

**Makes 12**

**1**

Preheat the oven to 230°C / 450°F /
Gas Mark 8. Sift the flour, baking powder,
mustard powder and salt into a mixing bowl.
Add the butter and rub it into the flour
mixture until the mixture resembles
breadcrumbs. Stir in 50 g / 2 oz of the cheese.

**2**

Make a well in the centre and add the milk
and egg. Mix gently and then turn the
dough out on to a lightly floured surface.
Roll it out and cut it into triangles or squares.
Brush lightly with milk and sprinkle with
the remaining cheese. Leave to rest for
15 minutes, then bake them for 15 minutes,
or until well risen.

# Oatcakes

*These are very simple to make and are an excellent addition to a cheese board.*

### INGREDIENTS

*225 g / 8 oz / 1⅔ cups medium*
*oatmeal*
*75 g / 3 oz / ¾ cup plain flour*
*¼ tsp bicarbonate of soda*
*5 ml / 1 tsp salt*
*25 g / 1 oz / 2 tbsp hard white*
*vegetable fat*
*25 g / 1 oz / 2 tbsp butter*

**Makes 24**

**1**

Preheat the oven to 220°C / 425°F /
Gas Mark 7. Place the oatmeal, flour, soda
and salt in a large bowl. Gently melt
the two fats together in a pan.

**2**

Add the melted fat and enough boiling water
to make a soft dough. Turn out on to a
surface scattered with a little oatmeal.
Roll out the dough thinly and cut it into
circles. Bake the oatcakes on ungreased
baking trays for 15 minutes, until crisp.

# Blackberry Charlotte

*A classic pudding, perfect for cold days. Serve with lightly whipped cream or home-made custard.*

### INGREDIENTS

*65 g / 2½ oz / 5 tbsp unsalted butter*
*175 g / 6 oz / 3 cups fresh white breadcrumbs*
*50 g / 2 oz / 4 tbsp soft brown sugar*
*60 ml / 4 tbsp golden syrup*
*finely grated rind and juice of 2 lemons*
*50 g / 2 oz walnut halves*
*450 g / 1 lb blackberries*
*450 g / 1 lb cooking apples, peeled, cored and finely sliced*

**Serves 4**

1

Preheat the oven to 180°C / 350°F / Gas Mark 4. Grease a 450 ml / ¾ pint / 2 cup dish with 15 g / ½ oz / 1 tbsp of the butter. Melt the remaining butter and add the breadcrumbs. Sauté them for 5–7 minutes, until the crumbs are a little crisp and golden. Leave to cool slightly.

2

Place the sugar, syrup, lemon rind and juice in a small saucepan and gently warm them. Add the crumbs.

3

Process the walnuts until they are finely ground.

4

Arrange a thin layer of blackberries on the dish. Top with a thin layer of crumbs.

5

Add a thin layer of apple, topping it with another thin layer of crumbs. Repeat the process with another layer of blackberries, followed by a layer of crumbs. Continue until you have used up all the ingredients, finishing with a layer of crumbs.

The mixture should be piled well above the top edge of the dish, because it shrinks during cooking. Bake for 30 minutes, until the crumbs are golden and the fruit is soft.

# Poached Pears

*Serve warm with clotted cream and crisp shortbread fingers.*

### INGREDIENTS

*6 medium pears*
*350 g / 12 oz / 1¾ cups caster*
*sugar*
*75 ml / 5 tbsp runny honey*
*1 vanilla pod*
*600 ml / 1 pint / 2½ cups red wine*
*5 ml / 1 tsp whole cloves*
*7 cm / 3 in cinnamon stick*

**Serves 4**

### 1

Peel the pears but leave them whole,
keeping the stalks as well.

### 2

Put the sugar, honey, vanilla pod, wine,
cloves and cinnamon stick in a large pan.

### 3

Add the pears and poach until soft, about
30 minutes. When the pears are tender,
remove them with a slotted spoon and keep
them warm. Remove the vanilla pod, cloves
and cinnamon stick and boil the liquid
until it is reduced by half. Serve spooned
over the pears.

# Steamed Ginger and Cinnamon Syrup Pudding

*A traditional and comforting steamed pudding, best served with custard.*

## INGREDIENTS

120 g / 4½ oz / 9 tbsp softened
butter
45 ml / 3 tbsp golden syrup
115 g / 4 oz / ½ cup caster sugar
2 eggs, lightly beaten
115 g / 4 oz / 1 cup plain flour
5 ml / 1 tsp baking powder
5 ml / 1 tsp ground cinnamon
25 g / 1 oz stem ginger,
finely chopped
30 ml / 2 tbsp milk

**Serves 4**

### 1

Set a full steamer or saucepan of water on to boil. Lightly grease a 600 ml / 1 pint / 2½ cup pudding basin with 15 g / ½ oz / 1 tbsp butter. Place the golden syrup in the basin.

### 2

Cream the remaining butter and sugar together until light and fluffy. Gradually add the eggs until the mixture is glossy. Sift the flour, baking powder and cinnamon together and fold them into the mixture, with the stem ginger. Add the milk to make a soft, dropping consistency.

### 3

Spoon the batter into the basin and smooth the top. Cover with a pleated piece of greaseproof paper, to allow for expansion during cooking. Tie securely with string and steam for 1½–2 hours, making sure that the water level is kept topped up, to ensure a good flow of steam to cook the pudding. Turn the pudding out to serve it.

# French Apple Tart

*For added flavour, scatter some toasted, flaked almonds over the top of this classic tart.*

### INGREDIENTS

**For the pastry**
*115 g / 4 oz / ½ cup unsalted
butter, softened
50 g / 2 oz / 4 tbsp vanilla sugar
1 egg
225 g / 8 oz / 2 cups plain flour*

**For the filling**
*50 g / 2 oz / 4 tbsp unsalted butter
5 large tart apples, peeled, cored
and sliced
juice of ½ lemon
300 ml / ½ pint / 1¼ cups double
cream
2 egg yolks
25 g / 1 oz / 2 tbsp vanilla sugar
50 g / 2 oz / ⅔ cup ground
almonds, toasted
25 g / 1 oz / 2 tbsp flaked almonds,
toasted, to garnish*

**Serves 8**

1

Place the butter and sugar in a food processor and process them well together. Add the egg and process to mix it in well.

2

Add the flour and process till you have a soft dough. Wrap the dough in cling film and chill it for 30 minutes.

3

Roll the pastry out on a lightly floured surface to about 22–25 cm / 9–10 in diameter.

4

Line a flan tin with the pastry and chill it for a further 30 minutes. Preheat the oven to 220°C / 425°F / Gas Mark 7 and place a baking sheet in the oven to heat up. Line the pastry case with greaseproof paper and baking beans and bake blind on the baking sheet for 10 minutes. Then remove the beans and paper and cook for a further 5 minutes.

5

Turn the oven down to 190°C / 375°F / Gas Mark 5. To make the filling, melt the butter in a frying pan and lightly sauté the apples for 5–7 minutes. Sprinkle the apples with lemon juice.

6

Beat the cream and egg yolks with the sugar. Stir in the toasted ground almonds. Arrange the apple slices on top of the warm pastry and pour over the cream mixture. Bake for 25 minutes, or until the cream is just about set – it tastes better if the cream is still slightly runny in the centre. Serve hot or cold, scattered with flaked almonds.

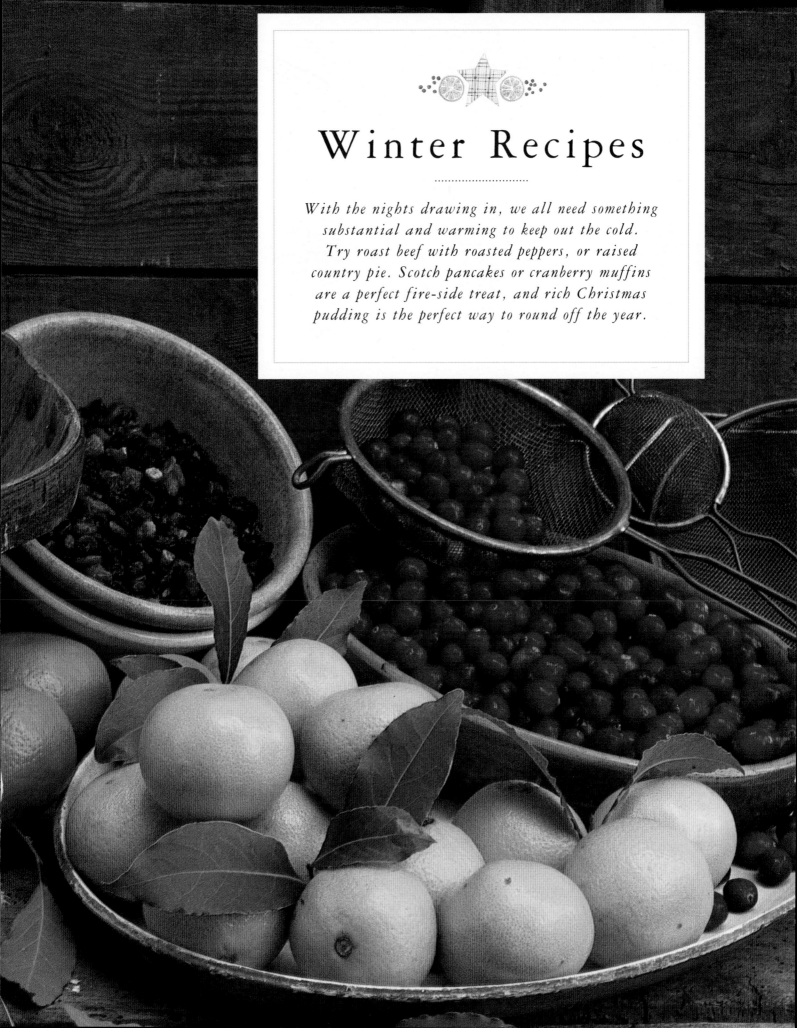

# Winter Recipes

With the nights drawing in, we all need something
substantial and warming to keep out the cold.
Try roast beef with roasted peppers, or raised
country pie. Scotch pancakes or cranberry muffins
are a perfect fire-side treat, and rich Christmas
pudding is the perfect way to round off the year.

# Roast Beef with Porcini and Roasted Sweet Peppers

*A substantial and warming dish for cold, dark evenings.*

<u>INGREDIENTS</u>

*1.5 kg / 3–3½ lb piece of sirloin*
*15 ml / 1 tbsp olive oil*
*450 g / 1 lb small red peppers*
*115 g / 4 oz mushrooms*
*175 g / 6 oz thick-sliced pancetta*
*or smoked bacon, cubed*
*50 g / 2 oz / 2 tbsp plain flour*
*150 ml / ¼ pint / ⅔ cup full-*
*bodied red wine*
*300 ml / ½ pint / 1¼ cups beef stock*
*30 ml / 2 tbsp Marsala*
*10 ml / 2 tsp dried mixed herbs*
*salt and freshly ground*
*black pepper*

**Serves 8**

1

Preheat the oven to 190°C / 375°F / Gas Mark 5. Season the meat well. Heat the olive oil in a large frying pan. When very hot, brown the meat on all sides. Place in a large roasting tin and cook for 1¼ hours.

2

Put the red peppers in the oven to roast for 20 minutes, if small ones are available, or 45 minutes if large ones are used.

3

Near the end of the meat's cooking time, prepare the gravy. Roughly chop the mushroom caps and stems.

4

Heat the frying pan again and add the pancetta or bacon. Cook until the fat runs freely from the meat. Add the flour and cook for a few minutes until browned.

5

Gradually stir in the red wine and the stock. Bring to the boil, stirring. Lower the heat and add the Marsala, herbs and seasoning.

6

Add the mushrooms to the pan and heat through. Remove the sirloin from the oven and leave to stand for 10 minutes before carving it. Serve with the roasted peppers and the hot gravy.

# Bacon and Lentil Soup

*Serve this hearty soup with chunks of warm, crusty bread.*

### INGREDIENTS

*450 g / 1 lb thick-sliced
bacon, cubed
1 onion, roughly chopped
1 small turnip, roughly chopped
1 celery stick, chopped
1 carrot, sliced
1 potato, peeled and
roughly chopped
75 g / 3 oz / ½ cup lentils
1 bouquet garni
freshly ground black pepper*

**Serves 4**

1

Heat a large pan and add the bacon. Cook for a few minutes, allowing the fat to run out.

2

Add all the vegetables and cook for 4 minutes.

3

Add the lentils, bouquet garni, seasoning and enough water to cover. Bring to the boil and simmer for 1 hour, or until the lentils are tender.

# Creamy Layered Potatoes

*Cook the potatoes on the hob first to help the dish to bake more quickly.*

## INGREDIENTS

*1.5 kg / 3–3½ lb large potatoes,
peeled and sliced
2 large onions, sliced
75 g / 3 oz / 6 tbsp unsalted butter
300 ml / ½ pint / 1¼ cups double
cream
salt and freshly ground
black pepper*

**Serves 6**

1

Preheat the oven to 200°C / 400°F /
Gas Mark 6. Blanch the sliced potatoes for 2
minutes, and drain well. Place the potatoes,
onions, butter and cream in a large pan,
stir well and cook for about 15 minutes.

2

Transfer to an ovenproof dish, season and
bake for 1 hour, until the potatoes are tender.

# Traditional Beef Stew and Dumplings

*This dish can cook in the oven while you go for a wintery walk to work up an appetite.*

### INGREDIENTS

*25 g / 1 oz / 1 tbsp plain flour*
*1.2 kg / 2½ lb stewing steak,*
*cubed*
*30 ml / 2 tbsp olive oil*
*2 large onions, sliced*
*450 g / 1 lb carrots, sliced*
*300 ml / ½ pint / 1¼ cups*
*Guinness or dark beer*
*3 bay leaves*
*10 ml / 2 tsp brown sugar*
*3 fresh thyme sprigs*
*5 ml / 1 tsp cider vinegar*
*salt and freshly ground*
*black pepper*

For the dumplings
*115 g / 4 oz / ½ cup grated hard*
*white fat*
*225 g / 8 oz / 2 cups self-raising*
*flour*
*30 ml / 2 tbsp chopped mixed*
*fresh herbs*
*about 150 ml / ¼ pint / ⅔ cup*
*water*

**Serves 6**

### 1

Preheat the oven to 160°C / 325°F /
Gas Mark 3. Season the flour and sprinkle
over the meat, tossing to coat.

### 2

Heat the oil in a large casserole and lightly
sauté the onions and carrots. Remove the
vegetables with a slotted spoon and
reserve them.

### 3

Brown the meat well in batches
in the casserole.

### 4

Return all the vegetables to the casserole and
add any leftover seasoned flour. Add the
Guinness or beer, bay leaves, sugar and
thyme. Bring the liquid to the boil and then
transfer to the oven. Leave the meat to cook
for 1 hour and 40 minutes, before making
the dumplings.

### 5

Mix the grated fat, flour and herbs together.
Add enough water to make a soft
sticky dough.

### 6

Form the dough into small balls with floured
hands. Add the cider vinegar to the meat and
spoon the dumplings on top. Cook for a
further 20 minutes, until the dumplings
have cooked through, and serve hot.

# Country Pie

*A classic raised pie. It takes quite a long time to make,*
*but is a perfect winter treat.*

INGREDIENTS

*1 small duck*
*1 small chicken*
*350 g / 12 oz pork belly, minced*
*1 egg, lightly beaten*
*2 shallots, finely chopped*
*½ tsp ground cinnamon*
*½ tsp grated nutmeg*
*5 ml / 1 tsp Worcestershire sauce*
*finely grated rind of 1 lemon*
*½ tsp freshly ground black pepper*
*150 ml / ¼ pint / ⅔ cup red wine*
*175 g / 6 oz ham, cut into cubes*
*salt and freshly ground*
*black pepper*

*For the jelly*
*all the meat bones and trimmings*
*2 carrots*
*1 onion*
*2 celery sticks*
*15 ml / 1 tbsp red wine*
*1 bay leaf*
*1 whole clove*
*1 sachet of gelatine*
*(about 15 g / 1 oz)*

*For the pastry*
*225 g / 8 oz / 1 cup hard white fat*
*300 ml / ½ pint / 1¼ cups boiling*
*water*
*675 g / 1½ lb / 6 cups plain flour*
*1 egg, lightly beaten with a*
*pinch of salt*

**Serves 12**

1

Cut as much meat from the raw duck and chicken as possible, removing the skin and sinews. Cut the duck and chicken breasts into cubes and set them aside.

2

Mix the rest of the duck and chicken meat with the minced pork, egg, shallots, spices, Worcestershire sauce, lemon rind and salt and pepper. Add the red wine and leave for about 15 minutes for the flavours to develop.

3

To make the jelly, place the meat bones and trimmings, carrots, onion, celery, wine, bay leaf and clove in a large pan and cover with 2.75 litres / 5 pints / 12½ cups of water. Bring to the boil, skimming off any scum, and simmer gently for 2½ hours.

4

To make the pastry, place the fat and water in a pan and bring to the boil. Sieve the flour and a pinch of salt into a bowl and pour on the liquid. Mix with a wooden spoon, and, when the dough is cool enough to handle, knead it well and let it sit in a warm place, covered with a cloth, for 20–30 minutes or until you are ready to use it. Preheat the oven to 200°C / 400°F / Gas Mark 6.

### 5

Grease a 25 cm / 10 in loose-based deep cake tin. Roll out about two-thirds of the pastry thinly enough to line the cake tin. Make sure there are no holes and allow enough pastry to leave a little hanging over the top. Fill the pie with a layer of half the minced-pork mixture; then top this with a layer of the cubed duck and chicken breast-meat and cubes of ham. Top with the remaining minced pork. Brush the overhanging edges of pastry with water and cover with the remaining rolled-out pastry. Seal the edges well. Make two large holes in the top and decorate with any pastry trimmings.

### 6

Bake the pie for 30 minutes. Brush the top with the egg and salt mixture. Turn down the oven to 180°C / 350°F / Gas Mark 4. After 30 minutes loosely cover the pie with foil to prevent the top getting too brown, and bake it for a further 1 hour.

### 7

Strain the stock after 2½ hours. Let it cool and remove the solidified layer of fat from the surface. Measure 600 ml / 1 pint / 2½ cups of stock. Heat it gently to just below boiling point and whisk the gelatine into it until no lumps are left. Add the remaining strained stock and leave to cool.

### 8

When the pie is cool, place a funnel through one of the holes and pour in as much of the stock as possible, letting it come up to the holes in the crust. Leave to set for at least 24 hours before slicing and serving.

# Leek and Onion Tart

*This unusual recipe isn't a normal tart with pastry, but an all-in-one savoury slice that is excellent served as an accompaniment to roast meat.*

### INGREDIENTS

50 g / 2 oz / 4 tbsp unsalted butter
350 g / 12 oz leeks, sliced thinly
225 g / 8 oz / 2 cups self-raising flour
115 g / 4 oz / ½ cup grated hard white fat
150 ml / ¼ pint / ⅔ cup water
salt and freshly ground black pepper

**Serves 4**

1

Preheat the oven to 200°C / 400°F / Gas Mark 6. Melt the butter in a pan and sauté the leeks until soft. Season well.

2

Mix the flour, fat and water together in a bowl to make a soft but sticky dough. Mix into the leek mixture in the pan. Place in a greased shallow ovenproof dish and bake for 30 minutes, or until brown and crispy. Serve sliced, as a vegetable accompaniment.

# Orange Shortbread Fingers

*These are a real tea-time treat. The fingers will keep in an airtight tin for up to two weeks.*

### INGREDIENTS

*115 g / 4 oz / ½ cup unsalted butter, softened*
*50 g / 2 oz / 4 tbsp caster sugar, plus a little extra*
*finely grated rind of 2 oranges*
*175 g / 6 oz / 1½ cups plain flour*

**Makes 18**

**1**

Preheat the oven to 190°C / 375°F / Gas Mark 5. Beat the butter and sugar together until they are soft and creamy. Beat in the orange rind.

**2**

Gradually add the flour and gently pull the dough together to form a soft ball. Roll the dough out on a lightly floured surface until about 1 cm / ½ in thick. Cut it into fingers, sprinkle over a little extra caster sugar, prick with a fork and bake for about 20 minutes, or until the fingers are a light golden colour.

# Cranberry Muffins

*A tea or breakfast dish that is not too sweet.*

## INGREDIENTS

*350 g / 12 oz / 3 cups plain flour*
*15 ml / 1 tsp baking powder*
*pinch of salt*
*115 g / 4 oz / ½ cup caster sugar*
*2 eggs*
*150 ml / ¼ pint / ⅔ cup milk*
*50 ml / 2 fl oz / 4 tbsp corn oil*
*finely grated rind of 1 orange*
*150 g / 5 oz cranberries*

**Makes 12**

### 1

Preheat the oven to 190°C / 375°F / Gas Mark 5. Line 12 deep muffin tins with paper cases. Mix the flour, baking powder, salt and caster sugar together.

### 2

Lightly beat the eggs with the milk and oil. Add them to the dry ingredients and blend to make a smooth batter. Stir in the orange rind and cranberries. Divide the mixture between the muffin cases and bake for 25 minutes until risen and golden. Leave to cool in the tins for a few minutes, and serve warm or cold.

# Scotch Pancakes

*Serve these while still warm, with butter and jam.*

## INGREDIENTS

*225 g / 8 oz / 2 cups self-raising flour*
*50 g / 2 oz / 4 tbsp caster sugar*
*50 g / 2 oz / 4 tbsp butter, melted*
*1 egg*
*300 ml / ½ pint / 1¼ cups milk*
*15 g / ½ oz / 1 tbsp hard white fat*

**Makes 24**

### 1

Mix the flour and sugar together. Add the melted butter and egg with two-thirds of the milk. Mix to a smooth batter – it should be thin enough to find its own level.

### 2

Heat a griddle or a heavy-based frying pan and wipe it with a little hard white fat. When hot, drop spoonfuls of the mixture on to the hot griddle or pan. When bubbles come to the surface of the pancakes, flip them over to cook until golden on the other side. Keep the pancakes warm wrapped in a tea towel while cooking the rest of the mixture.

# Christmas Pudding

*The classic Christmas dessert. Wrap it in muslin and store it in an airtight container for up to a year for the flavours to develop.*

### INGREDIENTS

*115 g / 4 oz / 1 cup plain flour*
*pinch of salt*
*5 ml / 1 tsp ground mixed spice*
*1/2 tsp ground cinnamon*
*1/4 tsp freshly grated nutmeg*
*225 g / 8 oz / 1 cup grated hard white fat*
*1 dessert apple, grated*
*225 g / 8 oz / 2 cups fresh white breadcrumbs*
*350 g / 12 oz / 1 7/8 cups soft brown sugar*
*50 g / 2 oz flaked almonds*
*225 g / 8 oz / 1 1/2 cups seedless raisins*
*225 g / 8 oz / 1 1/2 cups currants*
*225 g / 8 oz / 1 1/2 cups sultanas*
*115 g / 4 oz ready-to-eat dried apricots*
*115 g / 4 oz / 3/4 cup chopped mixed peel*
*finely grated rind and juice of 1 lemon*
*30 ml / 2 tbsp black treacle*
*3 eggs*
*300 ml / 1/2 pint / 1 1/4 cups milk*
*30 ml / 2 tbsp rum*

**Serves 8**

**1**

Sieve the flour, salt and spices into a large bowl.

**2**

Add the fat, apple and other dry ingredients, including the grated lemon rind.

**3**

Heat the treacle until warm and runny and pour into the dry ingredients.

**4**

Mix together the eggs, milk, rum and lemon juice.

**5**

Stir the liquid into the dry mixture.

**6**

Spoon the mixture into two 1.2 litre / 2 pint / 5 cup basins. Overwrap the puddings with pieces of greaseproof paper, pleated to allow for expansion, and tie with string. Steam the puddings in a steamer or saucepan of boiling water. Each pudding needs 10 hours' cooking and 3 hours' reheating. Remember to keep the water level topped up to keep the pans from boiling dry. Serve decorated with holly.

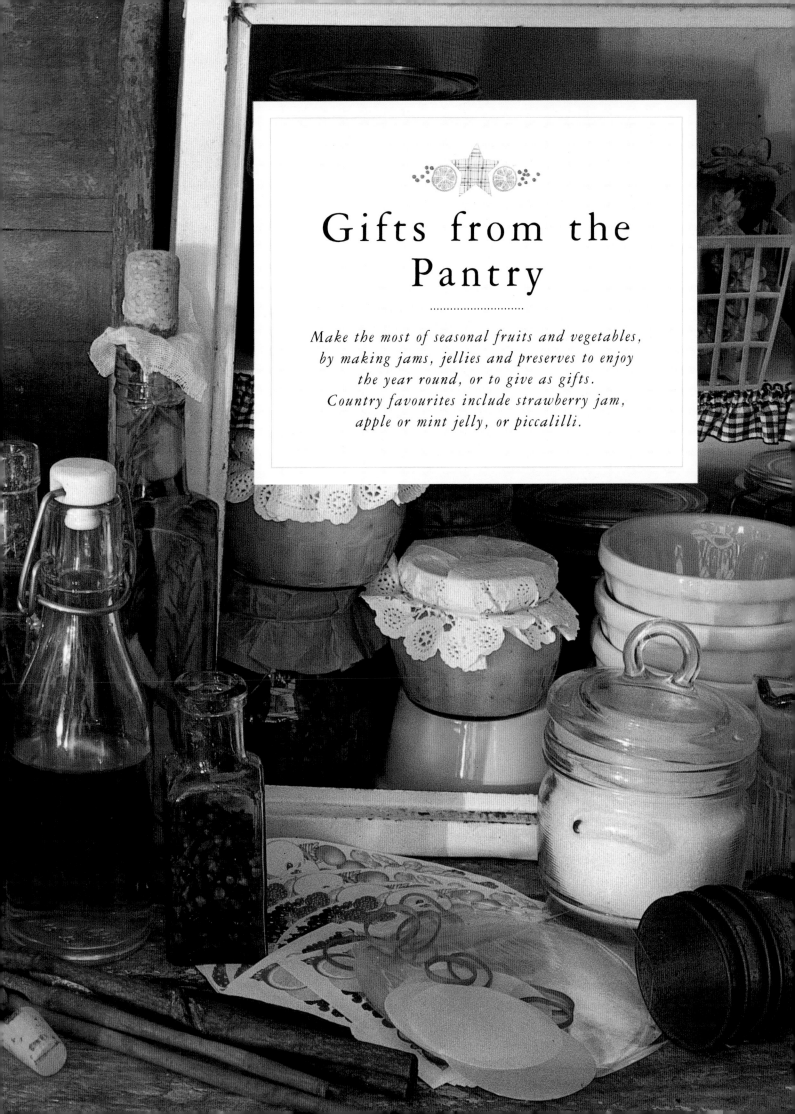

# Gifts from the Pantry

........................

*Make the most of seasonal fruits and vegetables,
by making jams, jellies and preserves to enjoy
the year round, or to give as gifts.
Country favourites include strawberry jam,
apple or mint jelly, or piccalilli.*

# Apple and Mint Jelly

*This jelly is delicious served with garden peas, as well as the more traditional rich roasted meat such as lamb.*

### INGREDIENTS

*900 g / 2 lb Bramley cooking apples*
*granulated sugar*
*45 ml / 3 tbsp chopped fresh mint*

**Makes 3 × 450 g / 1 lb jars**

**1**

Chop the apples roughly and put them in a preserving pan.

**2**

Add enough water to cover. Simmer until the fruit is soft.

**3**

Pour through a jelly bag, allowing it to drip overnight. Do not squeeze the bag or the jelly will become cloudy.

**4**

Measure the amount of juice. To every 600 ml / 1 pint / 2½ cups of juice, add 500 g / 1¼ lb / 2¾ cups granulated sugar.

**5**

Place the juice and sugar in a large pan and heat gently. Dissolve the sugar and then bring to the boil. Test for setting, by pouring about 15 ml / 1 tbsp into a saucer and leaving to cool slightly. If a wrinkle forms on the surface when pushed with a fingertip, the jelly will set. When a set is reached, leave to cool.

**6**

Stir in the mint and pot into sterilized jars. Seal each jar with a waxed disc and a tightly fitting cellophane top. Store in a cool, dark place. The jelly will keep unopened for up to a year. Once opened, keep in the fridge and consume within a week.

# Lemon and Lime Curd

*Serve this creamy, tangy spread with toast or muffins, instead of jam, for a delightful change.*

## INGREDIENTS

*115 g / 4 oz / ½ cup unsalted butter*
*3 eggs*

*grated rind and juice of 2 lemons*
*grated rind and juice of 2 limes*
*225 g / 8 oz / 1⅛ cups caster sugar*

**Makes 2 × 450g / 1 lb jars**

### 1

Set a heatproof mixing bowl over a large pan of simmering water. Add the butter.

### 2

Lightly beat the eggs and add them to the butter.

### 3

Add the lemon and lime rinds and juices, then add the sugar.

### 4

Stir the mixture constantly until it thickens. Pour into sterilized jars. Seal each jar with a waxed disc and a tightly fitting cellophane top. Store in a cool, dark place. The curd will keep unopened for up to a month. Once opened, keep in the fridge and consume within a week.

# Poached Spiced Plums in Brandy

*Bottling spiced fruit is a great way to preserve summer flavours for eating in winter. Serve these with whipped cream as a dessert.*

INGREDIENTS

600 ml / 1 pint / 2½ cups brandy
rind of 1 lemon, peeled in a
long strip
350 g / 12 oz / 1⅔ cups
caster sugar
1 cinnamon stick
900 g / 2 lb fresh plums

**Makes 900 g / 2 lb**

1

Put the brandy, lemon rind, sugar and cinnamon stick in a large pan and heat gently to dissolve the sugar. Add the plums and poach for 15 minutes, or until soft. Remove with a slotted spoon.

2

Reduce the syrup by a third by rapid boiling. Strain it over the plums. Bottle the plums in large sterilized jars. Seal tightly and store for up to 6 months in a cool, dark place.

# Spiced Pickled Pears

*These delicious pears are the perfect accompaniment for cooked ham or cold meat salads.*

### INGREDIENTS

*900 g / 2 lb pears*
*600 ml / 1 pint / 2½ cups*
*white-wine vinegar*
*225 g / 8 oz / 1⅛ cups caster sugar*
*1 cinnamon stick*
*5 star anise*
*10 whole cloves*

**Makes 900 g / 2 lb**

1

Peel the pears, keeping them whole
and leaving on the stalks. Heat the vinegar
and sugar together until the sugar has melted.
Pour over the pears and poach for 15 minutes.

2

Add the cinnamon, star anise and cloves
and simmer for 10 minutes. Remove the
pears and pack tightly into sterilized jars.
Simmer the syrup for a further 15 minutes
and pour it over the pears. Seal the jars
tightly and store in a cool, dark place. The
pears will keep for up to a year unopened.
Once opened, store in the fridge and
consume within a week.

GIFTS FROM THE PANTRY

# Tomato Chutney

*This spicy chutney is delicious with a selection of cheeses and biscuits,*
*or with cold meats.*

INGREDIENTS

900 g / 2 lb tomatoes, skinned
225 g / 8 oz / 1⅓ cups raisins
225 g / 8 oz onions, chopped

225 g / 8 oz / 1⅛ cups caster sugar
600 ml / 1 pint / 2½ cups
malt vinegar

**Makes 4 × 450g / 1 lb jars**

### 1

Chop the tomatoes roughly. Put them in
a preserving pan.

### 2

Add the raisins, onions and caster sugar.

### 3

Pour over the vinegar. Bring to the boil
and let it simmer for 2 hours, uncovered.
Pot into sterilized jars. Seal with a waxed disc
and cover with a tightly fitting cellophane
top. Store in a cool, dark place. The chutney
will keep unopened for up to a year. Once
opened, store in the fridge and consume
within a week.

# Strawberry Jam

*This classic recipe is always popular. Make sure the jam is allowed to cool before pouring into jars so the fruit doesn't float to the top.*

### INGREDIENTS

*1.5 kg / 3–3½ lb strawberries*
*juice of ½ lemon*
*1.5 kg / 3–3½ lb granulated sugar*

**Makes about 2.25 kg / 5 lb**

**1**

Hull the strawberries.

**2**

Put the strawberries in a pan with the lemon juice. Mash a few of the strawberries. Let the fruit simmer for 20 minutes or until softened.

**3**

Add the sugar and let it dissolve slowly over a gentle heat. Then let the jam boil rapidly until a setting point is reached.

**4**

Leave to stand until the strawberries are well distributed through the jam. Pot into sterilized jars. Seal each jar with a waxed disc and cover with a tightly fitting cellophane top. Store in a cool dark place. The jam may be kept unopened for up to a year. Once opened, keep in the fridge and consume within a week.

# Three-fruit Marmalade

*Home-made marmalade may be time-consuming but the results are incomparably better than store-bought varieties.*

### INGREDIENTS

350 g / 12 oz oranges
350 g / 12 oz lemons
700 g / 1½ lb grapefruit
2.5 litres / 4½ pints / 10¼ cups
water
2.75 kg / 6 lb granulated sugar
**Makes 6 × 450 g / 1 lb jars**

1

Rinse and dry the fruit.

2

Put the fruit in a preserving pan. Add the water and let it simmer for about 2 hours.

3

Quarter the fruit, remove the pulp and add it to the pan with the cooking liquid.

4

Cut the rinds into slivers, and add to the pan. Add the sugar. Gently heat until the sugar has dissolved. Bring to the boil and cook until a setting point is reached. Leave to stand for 1 hour to allow the peel to settle. Pour into sterilized jars. Seal each jar with a waxed disc and a tightly fitting cellophane top. Store in a cool, dark place.

# Piccalilli

*The piquancy of this relish partners well with sausages, bacon or ham.*

### INGREDIENTS

675 g / 1½ lb cauliflower
450 g / 1 lb small onions
350 g / 12 oz French beans
5 ml / 1 tsp ground turmeric

5 ml / 1 tsp dry mustard powder
10 ml / 2 tsp cornflour
600 ml / 1 pint / 2½ cups vinegar

**Makes 3 × 450 g / 1 lb jars**

### 1

Cut the cauliflower into tiny florets.

### 2

Peel the onions and top and tail
the French beans.

### 3

In a small saucepan, measure in the turmeric,
mustard powder and cornflour, and pour
over the vinegar. Stir well and simmer
for 10 minutes.

### 4

Pour the vinegar mixture over the vegetables
in a pan, mix well and simmer
for 45 minutes.

### 5

Pour into sterilized jars. Seal each jar with a
waxed disc and a tightly fitting cellophane
top. Store in a cool dark place. The piccalilli
will keep unopened for up to a year. Once
opened store in the fridge and consume
within a week.

# Rosemary-flavoured Oil

*This pungent oil is ideal drizzled over meat or vegetables before grilling.*

## INGREDIENTS

*600 ml / 1 pint / 2½ cups olive oil*
*5 fresh rosemary sprigs*

**Makes 600 ml / 1 pint / 2½ cups**

1

Heat the oil until warm but not too hot.

2

Add four rosemary sprigs and heat gently.
Put the reserved rosemary sprig in a clean
bottle. Strain the oil, pour in the bottle and
seal tightly. Allow to cool and store in a
cool, dark place. Use within a week.

# Thyme-flavoured Vinegar

*This vinegar is delicious sprinkled over salmon intended for poaching.*

## INGREDIENTS

*600 ml / 1 pint / 2½ cups*
*white-wine vinegar*
*5 fresh thyme sprigs*
*3 garlic cloves, peeled*

**Makes 600 ml / 1 pint / 2½ cups**

1

Warm the vinegar.

2

Add four thyme sprigs and the garlic and
heat gently. Put the reserved thyme sprig in
a clean bottle, strain the vinegar, and add to
the bottle. Seal tightly, allow to cool and
store in a cool, dark place. The vinegar
may be kept unopened for up to 3 months.

# Index

# INDEX

# Acknowledgements

Tessa Evelegh would like to thank Lindsay Porter for all her inspiration and encouragement in putting this book together, *Practical Gardening* magazine for all their support, Michelle Garrett for her wonderful, vibrant photographs and James and Madeleine for their encouragement and friendship.

Tessa and the publishers would also like to thank Fiona Barnett at Manic Botanic for the wheat heart on page 120, Eileen Simpson at Hill Farm Herbs for supplying the dried-herb wreath on page 136 and Somerset House of Iron for the chair featured on the jacket. See *Suppliers* for addresses.

# Suppliers

Appalachia The Folk Art Shop,
14a George Street,
St Albans, Herts AL3 4ER;
Tel: 01727 836796; Fax: 01992 467560

Brats,
281 King's Road,
London SW3 5EW;
Tel: 0171-351 7674;
*also* 624c Fulham Road,
London SW6 5RS;
Tel: 0171 731 6915
(Suppliers of Mediterranean palette paints)

Farrow & Ball Ltd,
Madens Trading Estate,
Wimborne, Dorset BH21 7NL;
Tel: 01202 876141; Fax: 01202 873793
(Suppliers of National Trust paints)

Hill Farm Herbs,
Park Walk, Brigstock,
Northants NN14 3HH;
Tel: 01536 373694; Fax: 01536 373246
(potted fresh herbs, dried herbs and flowers, dried flower decorations).

Manic Botanic,
34 Juer Street,
London SW11 4RF;
Tel: 0171 978 4505
(made-to-order floral decorations).

Paint Magic,
79 Shepperton Road,
London N1 3DF
Tel: 0171 354 9696; Fax: 0171-226 7760
(Suppliers of paints and varnishes)

Shaker Ltd,
25 Harcourt Street,
London W1H 1DT;
*also* 322 King's Road,
London SW3 5UH.
Mail order to Harcourt Street address or by telephone on 0171 742 7672

Somerset House of Iron
779 Fulham Road,
London SW6 5HR;
Tel: 0171-371 0436

Robert Young Antiques,
68 Battersea Bridge Road,
London SW11 3AG;
Tel: 0171-228 7847